ADVANCE PRAISE

"Sylvia Ann Hewlett and Ripa Rashid deftly solve for the challenges of developing local talent to lead emerging market growth for multinationals. With survey data from eleven markets, their research sheds new light on what rising leaders need to know about projecting credibility at headquarters—and winning the sponsorship they'll need to break into the executive suite. I particularly appreciate the 'gender lens,' as growing female executives is an imperative for healthcare and insurance multinationals intent on harnessing the power of the purse globally."

—Mark T. Bertolini, *Chairman and CEO,*
Aetna Inc.

"*Growing Global Executives: The New Competencies* includes useful research and insight to guide current and aspiring business leaders in today's global economy. Sylvia Ann Hewlett and Ripa Rashid deconstruct the leadership challenges presented by cultural, generational, and gender differences, particularly for executives operating across borders, time zones, and distance. The authors provide sound advice on how to project credibility, build trust, communicate virtually, and develop talent across those differences in ways that will enable business success."

—Horacio D. Rozanski, *President and CEO,*
Booz Allen Hamilton

D1304307

"Grooming leaders who can engender confidence in the boardroom while effectively motivating coworkers across cultures and time zones is a major challenge for every multinational corporation. Here, armed with telling data drawn from major developed—as well as developing—markets, the authors ably dissect the nuances of culture, gender, and communication, which together, comprise a delicate balance of superior corporate leadership in the twenty-first century."

—Gregory J. Fleming, *President*, Morgan Stanley Wealth Management and Morgan Stanley Investment Management

"Sylvia Ann Hewlett and Ripa Rashid have written an insightful and thought-provoking guide on how to build effective, trusting, and mutually beneficial relationships within multinational corporations. Leaders who are committed to bridging the cultural divide will take away an actionable list of concrete steps they can take to increase their international reach. Enlivening robust data with stories from executives all over the world, Hewlett and Rashid make a clear and compelling case that inclusive leadership is good for business, both in terms of the bottom line and in encouraging worldwide employees to be more connected and innovative."

—John D. Finnegan, *Chairman, President, and CEO,* The Chubb Corporation

"Yet again, Sylvia Ann Hewlett and the Center for Talent Innovation have shone light on a little-researched and even less understood area of global leadership: the effective characteristics of leadership in different countries and cultures. The variety revealed in 'what works' is both striking and invaluable as we adapt our businesses and leadership practices to succeed in a global marketplace. The study goes beyond the intuitive, offering impactful anecdotes and quantitative research that combine to powerful effect."

—Helena Morrissey, CBE,
CEO, Newton Investments, and *Founder,* 30% Club

"Grooming the next generation of talent worldwide to be inclusive leaders is no easy task, but Sylvia Ann Hewlett and Ripa Rashid know just how to go about it. An energetic and engaging read, *Growing Global Executives* offers a whole new approach to multinationals' most critical talent challenge."

—Geri Thomas, *President of Georgia Market and Global Diversity & Inclusion Executive,* Bank of America Corporation

GROWING
GLOBAL
EXECUTIVES

THE NEW COMPETENCIES

GROWING
GLOBAL
EXECUTIVES

THE NEW COMPETENCIES

FOREWORD BY "TIGER" TYAGARAJAN

SYLVIA ANN HEWLETT
RIPA RASHID

A CENTER FOR TALENT INNOVATION PUBLICATION • NEW YORK, NY

This is a Center for Talent Innovation Publication

A Vireo Book | Rare Bird Books
453 South Spring Street, Suite 302
Los Angeles, CA 90013
rarebirdbooks.com

Copyright © 2015 by Center for Talent Innovation

FIRST TRADE PAPERBACK ORIGINAL EDITION

All rights reserved, including the right to reproduce this book or portions
thereof in any form whatsoever, including but not limited to print, audio, and
electronic. For more information, address:
A Vireo Book | Rare Bird Books Subsidiary Rights Department,
453 South Spring Street, Suite 302, Los Angeles, CA 90013.

Set in Minion
Printed in the United States

10 9 8 7 6 5 4 3 2 1

Publisher's Cataloging-in-Publication data

Hewlett, Sylvia Ann, 1946-
    Growing global executives : the new competencies / by Sylvia Ann Hewlett
and Ripa Rashid ; Foreword by "Tiger" Tyagarajan.
    pages cm
    ISBN 978-1-942600-48-0
    Includes bibliographical references and index.

1. Executives—Training of. 2. Executive ability. 3. Globalization. 4. Industrial
management. 5. Corporate governance. 6. International business enterprises—
Management. I. Rashid, Ripa. II. Tyagarajan, N.V. III. Title.

HD30.4 .H49 2015
658.4/07124—dc23

*To the amazing thought leaders who have been
at the heart of this research:*

ROHINI ANAND

ERIKA IRISH BROWN

CAROLINE CARR

GAIL FIERSTEIN

CASSANDRA FRANGOS

VALERIE GRILLO

ROSALIND HUDNELL

FRANCES G. LASERSON

PIYUSH MEHTA

SHARI SLATE

DAVID TAMBURELLI

KARYN TWARONITE

"TIGER" TYAGARAJAN

ELANA WEINSTEIN

ANRÉ WILLIAMS

MELINDA WOLFE

PROJECT TEAM

Research

Laura Sherbin, Director

Pooja Jain-Link

Charlene Thrope

Publications

Melinda Marshall, Director

Isis Fabian

Julia Taylor Kennedy

Anna Weerasinghe

Project Management

Jennifer Zephirin

Communications

Tai Wingfield, Director

Silvia Marte

CONTENTS

FOREWORD

When I became Genpact's chief executive officer in 2011, one of the first things I did was relocate our leadership to the countries where our clients were headquartered. We'd been operating from Gurgaon, India since our inception as a business unit of GE in 1998. But after we spun off in 2005, during the years that I was heading up sales and marketing, I realized that running a global services business was, for all practical purposes, serving our clients' strategic needs. I didn't need to be "at the factory;" I needed to be sitting in the markets. And if that was true for me, then it was true for my leaders.

Today, with more than sixty-five thousand employees serving clients in twenty-five countries, we are a truly global corporation. Half of our leadership sits in key markets around the world, up from 23 percent merely four years ago. Seven of us live and work in the US, as 60 percent of our revenue derives from multinationals headquartered here. That's a tremendous change given that four years ago we were considered an "Indian" company.

In fact, our evolution is one of our calling cards: because we're on this transformational journey, our clients look to us to guide their own. As international as they are, they look to us for new ideas on how to work globally. They're contending with constraints on growth that prompt them to reconsider their own operating models. To become more nimble, more responsive to shifting market dynamics, they wonder: Should they, too, shift their centers of gravity? What might be the optimal global business model? And what competencies might that model demand of both its teams and its leaders?

If we're able to show them the way, then it's because of our multicultural DNA. The company I joined in 1998 had a predominantly Indian workforce with leadership that grew up in India but whose culture was American. It bore the imprint of Jack Welch, whose books—particularly *Control Your Destiny*—had a profound impact on me (and, clearly, on my destiny). While known as a command-and-control leader, Jack was way ahead of the curve in terms of the culture he built, both at GE and its global subsidiaries. GE was one of the first American companies to enter growth markets with the intent of sourcing, developing, and empowering local talent; GE Capital recruited me, after all. And Jack was among the first to perceive the power of crowd-sourcing. He would get people into a room from ten different businesses who literally had no business talking to each other—an aircraft engine developer who had a PhD in materials science talking to an analyst who built risk models for credit cards— and by the end of the day, every one of those people would walk away having learned something. He called it "boundary-lessness," but it's what we recognize today as diversity of thought and perspective.

Whether our differences are functional or cultural, Jack intuited that harnessing them was the key to sustaining innovation and solving thorny problems.

Furthermore, Jack understood that building an innovative culture depended on people not just coming up with great ideas, but sharing them and copying them. He had no patience for leaders who suffered what he called NIH ("not invented here") syndrome, people who stonewalled innovation because the idea behind it didn't come from them or their team. So at GE Capital, if a leader hit upon an idea that wound up delivering value to the business, she'd be recognized, but if she took that idea and evangelized it across businesses so that every other leader copied it, she'd be rewarded. As a result, we had teams from different businesses who functioned as one team sharing a lot of best practices and learning from each other, boosting revenues for the firm overall. We drove that value hard; as CEO of our business, I drive it even harder, because being able to collaborate across business units serves us well as we seek to unlock value across cultures and time zones for our clients.

One of the more valuable lessons I took from my early career was the notion that a great leader is a great learner, and that what makes someone a great learner is curiosity. We have always moved young leaders across businesses, across functions, and across experiences, confident that if they were hungry enough to learn, they'd acquire what they needed to know in order to succeed. This is what allowed me, in fact, to go from sales to risk management. I came in to interview for the marketing job and halfway through the interview was offered a risk job. During the interview, I was asked, "How can you accept a job that's the opposite of what you came in for?" I said, "I am not here to interview for a job, I am here to interview for a career. I thought the entry point was marketing, but you've made clear the entry point is risk." That was the first of many job changes I was offered within GE Capital until I landed in the role that put me in charge of our global services business, which gave me exposure to all of GE's businesses and the diversity of its portfolio. One day I was working with aircraft engines, the next day with credit cards, then with leasing, and the fourth day with NBC. That cross-unit exposure, coupled with my own insatiable curiosity, is what ultimately prepared me to be a key leader at Genpact as an independent company in 2005 and to take it public in 2007.

Genpact's approach to global expansion isn't dissimilar: we source talent locally for our delivery centers, and groom these men and women to assume leadership beyond their borders in a few years. When we set up operations in Hungary, China, and Mexico, for example, we recruited people who understood that space—the talent available, the local culture— and knew how to scale it and make it successful. Then I moved leaders who had proven capable of driving value in other places (namely India) to oversee the new operation, seed our best practices, and develop the people we recruited. Today, some of those recruits are running those delivery centers; others have moved out of their markets into bigger roles in the firm. It's critical, I've learned, to grow leaders we identify in emerging markets by giving them platforms bigger than their markets, exposing them to people and leaders who operate in mature markets so they might learn from their experience and benefit from their sponsorship. We make a point, despite the cost, of rotating our leaders from small markets into bigger ones. From Romania, or from China, they pack their bags and move to India for a few months. That ensures, when they go back, that they have much better networks. You can't insist that an emerging leader build a network when you haven't provided the platform.

This holds true at the highest levels of our firm: each of my market leaders, irrespective of the size of their markets, has equal standing in the firm and equal voice at my table. On the face of it, this doesn't make sense: for us, the US market is three times the size of the European market. But I've learned that to grow our client base in places like Europe, Japan, and Australia, I've got to bring in big leaders who've established sizeable networks there, make them my direct reports, and give them the stature and attention they need to grow those markets.

Our journey, with regard to growing our pipeline of global executives, is far from over. We are not as diverse as we should be, nor as I would like us to be. We have enough programs to provide women in emerging markets the ladder they need to grow into senior leader positions: 70 percent of my Chinese leadership team are women, as are 60 percent to 70 percent of my eastern European leadership team. The US and India, however, are proving more difficult. The next frontier for us is making sure more of our highly qualified women in these markets get the platform, the visibility, and the sponsorship they need to grow beyond mid-senior levels.

Yet in terms of our evolution to a truly global company—one that is poised to identify and act upon market opportunities—I think we have journeyed far. I don't know what the world will look like in five years; I'm confident no CEO does. How, then, do I run the ship? I need to create nimbleness and agility, so that I can turn this ship on a dime in a nanosecond. Then, so I know in which direction to turn it, I am going to need an antenna, one that picks up signals one second before my competitors' antennae. That's all I need. And looking at Genpact today, I think we've got it: the culture we've built ensures our agility, and with our leaders sitting next to our clients, we have a finger directly on the pulse of the markets we serve. That's the combination that I think will prove most successful—not only for us, but for global organizations of the future.

—"Tiger" Tyagarajan
Chief Executive Officer and President
Genpact
August 2015

INTRODUCTION

In the wake of the earthquake that devastated Haiti in 2010, the American Red Cross collected $488 billion in aid worldwide—the largest outpouring of donations in its history. Its chief executive, Gail McGovern, unveiled plans to develop brand new communities as well as rebuild old ones; in the neighborhood of Campeche, the Red Cross pledged to build some seven hundred homes that would provide residents with basic sanitation, running water, and electricity.[1]

To date, as revealed by ProPublica and NPR in a joint investigation of the charity, none of the communities have taken shape. Campeche remains a garbage-strewn slum of rusted sheet-metal shacks. And of the one hundred thirty thousand homes the Red Cross claims to have built island-wide, only six can be documented.[2] Managed from the US, with staff on the ground consisting largely of Americans, the Red Cross' housing campaign foundered for lack of expertise, language skills, and experience in cutting through the red tape around land access. The $24 million Campeche strategy will be scuttled when the organization withdraws from Haiti in 2016.[3]

The squandering of $170 million in infrastructure capital, not to mention nearly half a billion in relief funding, underscores the single largest growth constraint on international organizations in the private as well as public sector: an anemic pipeline of locally sourced leaders. Emerging markets in the South and East stand poised to take center stage in the global economy within the next ten years, a shift that is expected to increase not just market potential, but also market competition.[4] To be effective in these growth hubs, multinational corporatons (MNCs) need local leaders to help them navigate the red tape of local government and the labyrinth of local business channels.[5] To wield a competitive edge for years to come, MNCs need talent with local market intelligence, men and women who can identify unmet needs because they've experienced them firsthand, and who can innovate solutions appropriate to meet them because they're intimately acquainted with local customs, preferences, and living conditions.[6]

Indeed, to foresee challenges or nimbly respond to crises, MNCs need lieutenants on the front lines who are empowered to act on their local intelligence. The Red Cross had very few. Leadership roles went to expats, whose compensation cost the organization three times what hiring a local would have cost. Given the security situation, separation from family, and the demanding nature of the work, turnover among the expats was high, creating chronic vacancies that added to the organization's paralysis on the ground. As one staffer observed, "Everything would take four times as long because it would be micromanaged from DC, and they had no development experience."[7]

MNCs are well aware that the expatriate management model is ill-suited to growing their footprint and market share—not to mention stupendously expensive. Even before the global financial crisis of 2008, they were scaling back on the recruitment and deployment of this talent brigade, replacing them with local nationals, third-country nationals (executives who are neither nationals of the host country nor the country in which their MNC is headquartered), and returning nationals. According to a survey conducted by the Association of Executive Search Consultants of hiring activities in China, India, Brazil, the Middle East, and Russia, only 12 percent of senior executives in those markets were expats in 2008, compared with 56 percent in 1998.[8] The decline of the expat has steepened in recent years—because companies now have to make social insurance contributions on behalf of their foreign workers, making hiring them prohibitively expensive.[9] Little wonder that 76 percent of senior executives polled by the UN said their organizations should invest in developing global leadership capabilities in emerging markets.[10]

Multinational organizations that managed to get out in front of this talent trend—that developed local talent into leaders with strategic decision-making capability—have realized dramatic results in terms of local market penetration. General Electric (GE) was one of them. Up until 2001, GE abided by conventional wisdom: R&D was centralized at headquarters in the US, and innovation for the developing world consisted largely of simplifying a product that had been successful in the West in order to sell it at a lower price point. The resulting "innovation" was often entirely inappropriate for the markets the company hoped to capture. For example, GE's cheaper, emerging-market version of the surgical C-arm—a heavy, high-cost imaging machine designed for use in hospital settings—fell flat in India, where the majority of healthcare is dispensed in rural clinics.[11] But Omar Ishrak, a Bangladeshi who became CEO of GE Healthcare's clinical systems unit in 2005, took a different approach: he empowered teams at the local level to innovate products attuned to the needs of clinicians operating on foot in remote areas where electricity couldn't be relied upon, serving patients who could not afford to travel to city centers.[12] The result: GE's wildly successful low-cost Electrocardiogram (ECG) MAC 400, a handheld, battery-operated heart monitoring device that sent readings by cellphone. Developed specifically for the Indian market by a team of India-based engineers and designers, it demonstrated the competitive edge bestowed on MNCs that decentralized operations to make their subsidiaries in growth hubs more autonomous.[13]

Yet even in the burgeoning tech sector, international firms have not readily decommissioned the mother ship. GE's headquarters continues to entrust execution, but not decision-making, to satellites in the developing world.[14] MNCs based in the US and UK in particular struggle to develop and promote talent in the South and East beyond the director level.[15] They also struggle to deploy and incentivize homegrown talent to win business and satisfy clients abroad.[16]

Committed to diversifying their leadership pipeline, they have invested billions ($14 billion in the US alone)[17] in cultural competency training, multicultural leadership development, ex-pat executive coaching, and cultural navigation tools. Tools such as the ITAP International's Culture in the Workplace Questionnaire™[18] and Aperian Global's GlobeSmart® Teaming Assessment and Global Teams Online® e-training tool[19] (among numerous others[20]) have been developed on the basis of decades of research, including Geert Hofsted's groundbreaking theory of "bilateral leadership," the ten-year GLOBE study of sixty-two cultures, Richard Lewis' *When Cultures Collide*, and Erin Meyer's excellent *The Culture Map*, as well as more recent contributions to the field, such as Ernest Gundling's *Working Globesmart*.[21]

But these leadership development strategies ultimately fall short of growing locals into global executives because they fail to move candidates beyond *understanding* cultural differences to *acting* on them.[22] Local talent still lacks credibility with senior management at headquarters; expats still lack the culturally appropriate behaviors to create the partnerships and pathways necessary to driving value in the footprint; and senior managers continue to see and sponsor the people who surround them at headquarters, ensuring that the upper echelons of leadership resist diversification from abroad.[23] Distance and difference remain chasms for companies whose competitive success depends on bridging them.

Virtual communication platforms have indisputably helped bridge these divides. Recognizing the imperative of integrating information flow across a wide range of digital platforms and devices, and of growing innovative, responsive, and flexible global networks,[24] MNCs have been quick to prioritize investment in hardware, software, and training to facilitate virtual collaboration and knowledge sharing instead of other kinds of corporate development. A 2012 IBM study revealed that 71 percent of global CEOs see technology as the most critical factor in maintaining market competitiveness.[25] Towers Watson found that upward of 61 percent of MNCs plan to integrate mobile technology into existing systems.[26]

Yet even as technology eases communication and maximizes efficiencies, it introduces misunderstandings and productivity constraints. Corporate leaders must not only demonstrate high-level expertise in an ever-expanding array of complex digital technologies, but also project authority and unlock value in this virtual environment,[27] a challenge compounded by variances in quality and consistency due to inadequate infrastructure in the developing world.[28] Technological savvy, skillfulness in cross-cultural virtual team management, adroit use of mobile technology and social media, and better allocation of precious in-person time are critical to the success of global virtual team leaders, but guidance is scant and, as a result, success is mixed.[29]

What will it take to move more local talent into global leadership roles? How can MNCs unlock the innovative potential of local teams? What should be the focus of leadership development?

With this study, we answer these crucial questions. Drawing on an eleven-market quantitative sample (Brazil, China, Hong Kong, Japan, India, Russia, Singapore, South Africa, Turkey, the UK, and the US), interviews with forty-eight global executives, and focus groups with over fifty global team players, we find that emerging global leaders are in want of two core competencies: the ability to modify their leadership presence in order to project credibility to superiors at headquarters as well as to stakeholders worldwide, and the ability to unlock value from globally dispersed and culturally diverse teams through inclusive leadership. Overlooked by MNCs and business research organizations alike, these cutting-edge leadership competencies build on pioneering research of the Center for Talent Innovation (CTI), which shows how developing executive presence and inclusive leadership are the keys to growing executive potential in multicultural talent in US corporations.[30] On the global stage, we find these core competencies depend, respectively, on mastery of virtual communication, which enables emerging leaders to project credibility and leadership presence even when far from headquarters; and on sponsorship, which, as exclusive CTI research has demonstrated, generates high-level visibility for emerging leaders both as rising stars and as a developers of team talent.[31]

MNCs are grappling with a bewildering array of management issues today: the increasing economic clout of emerging markets, heightened competition for local talent, and an unprecedented dependence on virtual leadership have all contributed to sluggish revenues, uninspired business solutions, and stagnant talent pools. Yet these problems have a common solution: the innovative potential of emerging global leaders, gleaned from the ranks of the very MNCs facing these challenges. By tapping into this vastly underutilized resource, MNCs will not only jettison outmoded models of corporate leadership and gain a pipeline of diverse, innovative, and culturally savvy executives; they will also cement their competitive position in the world's fastest-growing marketplaces.

1

Projecting Credibility: Mastering the Double Pivot

What signals readiness for a global leadership role? An ability to project credibility to stakeholders around the world.

To be seen as having "the right stuff"—competence, confidence, and trustworthiness—leaders must exude executive presence: they must look, sound, and act in accordance with cultural expectations of authority figures. Research we conducted in 2012 on the "intangibles" of leadership shows that in the US, executive presence derives chiefly from gravitas, a constellation of behaviors that project credibility. Exhibiting calm in a crisis—"grace under fire"—tops the list of behaviors, followed by demonstrating decisiveness and integrity. Demonstrating emotional intelligence (EQ), establishing reputation and standing, and emanating charisma are other competencies that our research highlights as essential to being found credible as a leader in the US, whether you're male or female.

Globally, we find, gravitas is still the heart of the matter. According to 47 percent of respondents, gravitas is the most important component of a leader's executive presence (with communication skills and appearance—virtual and in-person—making up the rest).

Yet what our eleven-country dataset reveals about gravitas is that the behaviors that give rise to it are accorded different importance in different countries and regions. With the exception of demonstrating integrity, which respondents across markets prioritize in their leaders, gravitas varies from hemisphere to hemisphere, from country to country, and from corporate culture to corporate culture. If in US boardrooms it's essential to demonstrate authority, in Japan it's vital to show you can work across difference. In Russia, it's terribly important for leaders to first establish their reputation and status; in India, credibility derives from being able to inspire a following. Rising leaders must understand these cultural differences and adjust their gravitas accordingly to win the trust and respect of globally dispersed team members and clients as well as centrally located senior executives.

Projecting credibility thus becomes quite a challenge for leaders operating across time zones and cultures. Global leaders must master a double pivot, demonstrating authority with senior executives in the West (the vertical pivot) and prioritizing emotional intelligence with stakeholders in global markets (the horizontal pivot, which may well prove to be a multifaceted challenge).

PROJECTING CREDIBILITY: THE DOUBLE PIVOT

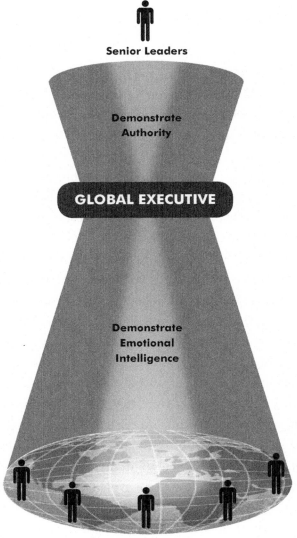

THE DOUBLE PIVOT

Makiko Eda, VP of Intel's Sales and Marketing Group and president of Intel Japan, is one such master pivoter. As a native of Japan, she enjoys working for a multinational company that respects her leadership skills and imbues her with authority—something that would never happen in a Japanese managerial hierarchy, where women are rarely welcome, she says. But she also enjoys, during her quarterly visits to Intel's headquarters in California, being "a translator of my culture to the Western world." Traveling between her office in Tokyo and Intel's operation in Santa Clara, she reflexively pivots, modifying her leadership style to project credibility in both environments.

"I do put on my cowboy hat at headquarters," she says. "People are debating: you have to participate. I'm not used to it; I'm used to being asked for my opinion, not to have to cut off people in order to interject it. But especially in topics where I'm assured of my expertise, I've learned to do it." Once back in Tokyo, however, she drops the combative style and resumes her respectful stance. "My reports tell me that it's a function of the language I'm speaking," Eda relates. "I'm very assertive and strong when I speak English; I'm very polite and soft when I speak Japanese." It's a linguistic difference, as well as a cultural one, she explains: English is more clear and direct in its word order, whereas there's more unspoken in Japanese; its very structure is indirect.

With her sales team and with clients throughout Asia, Eda adjusts her leadership style as local cultures dictate. With Koreans and Taiwanese, she works to coax out the unspoken in one-on-one conversations, as they rarely express their thoughts unbidden, and certainly won't share them on a big call. Whereas in India, where there's a culture of open debate—"each of them will have to say something about everything"—Eda asks clarifying questions and makes sure to hold individuals accountable. "India's a good example of where they're Asian but not my Asian," she explains. "Coming from Japan, from headquarters, I knew how they'd feel: there would be a battle for authority. ('She's never been to India and she's managing marketing!') So I have adopted an approach of total humility. 'Teach me, tell me why you do things that way,' is how I win their trust. It isn't my instinct, necessarily, but if I were them, that's what I would like to hear from my management."

Indeed, employing empathy—doing what Eda calls "the mind meld"—has served her extremely well in all local markets. "In instances where there's likely to be cultural tension, I try to get inside their psyches and simulate how they'll react in my head before I interact with them," she explains. "Then I ask questions; I show a willingness to learn." It's a tactic, she says, that has helped her bridge gender and age differences, as well as cultural differences. "Once I make it clear I'm not there to criticize or judge but to support them in the best possible way so that we can do the best possible job together—they trust me," she says. "Empathy works."

INTEGRITY

As Eda's story illustrates, the double pivot entails a seamless switch in gravitas. In general, we find, projecting credibility horizontally—to stakeholders across local markets—requires prioritizing emotional intelligence, whereas projecting credibility vertically (to those at headquarters) requires that one demonstrate authority.

In only one aspect of gravitas is pivoting unnecessary, and that's in demonstrating integrity. Integrity is table stakes. Unless you're seen as a person of your word—as someone who can be counted on to honor your commitments, no matter how onerous those may become—you won't get traction with any of the other behaviors. Globally dispersed team members won't go the extra mile for you because they don't believe you have their best interests at heart. Peers won't allocate work to your team or deliver resources that you request because they suspect your motives. Integrity is the foundation on which trust is built and relationships endure across both distance and difference. If you can't project it, you'll be incapable of driving results.

Integrity can take time to demonstrate. It often takes a crisis, as subordinates want to see not only how firmly you will stand in the face of a storm, but also whose interests you will shield. Nicolas Japy, CEO of

Remote Sites and Asia-Australia for Sodexo, describes being repeatedly tested: crises are perpetual because his people—some seventy thousand employees—are working under extreme circumstances in some of the world's most far-flung places, from the mountains of Afghanistan to the wilderness of Alaska. Japy depends on his on-site managers—who are fully empowered to hire, train, and deploy local talent, negotiate local partnerships, command resources, and otherwise do what's necessary to fulfill Sodexo's contract—to handle whatever comes up. Since the success of his division depends on these managers going the extra mile for him and the company, it's imperative that he demonstrate he will go the extra mile for them—quite literally. Japy tells of one such opportunity that he seized early in his global role when a site manager in New Caledonia, where Sodexo ran a camp serving a mining operation, called to tell him he had a crisis that he couldn't handle. "The client doesn't want to listen to me," the manager told him. "I don't know what to do." Japy, a French citizen who was working in central Africa at the time, got on a plane for the South Pacific. After two full days of travel, Japy arrived to learn that the client "didn't have the time" to meet with him. Japy went out to the camp to wait. Two days later, when the client showed up, Japy calmly told him that Sodexo could no longer do business with him. The client's deputy, sensing that Japy wasn't bluffing, quickly intervened to speak to him alone. Fifteen minutes later, Japy had what he came for: the client's commitment to honor Sodexo's terms of engagement. "That happened ten years ago, and my people on the ground are still talking about it: 'Nicolas flew twenty thousand kilometers, went to the campsite, and negotiated intensely with the client to sort it out.' And that site manager? He is still there working for me."

AUTHORITY VS. EQ

Our interviews with rising leaders and seasoned global executives make clear that what marks a leader as ready for global responsibility is knowing when to assert authority and when to demonstrate emotional intelligence. To put it another way, rising global leaders can't afford to misread context. A failure to adapt your style to the situation can undermine your credibility as a leader in irreparable ways.

Ron Lee, a managing director at Goldman Sachs who heads up its private wealth business in Asia, has had to learn the importance of the double pivot: having grown up in Ohio and spending the formative years of his career in New York, he has a cultural background helpful for communicating to the firm's senior leadership; and having spent the last twenty years living and working in Hong Kong and Singapore, he's acquired Asian cultural smarts (an acquisition aided by the fact that Lee is of Korean descent). So it fell to him, he says, to coach a colleague who struggled to project credibility with Goldman's senior leaders.

Lee gave his colleague an ideal forum in which to demonstrate his acumen and leadership: a convening of an important executive committee in Asia. But to Lee's disappointment, when the strategic group began discussing a topic with which his colleague was very familiar, he remained silent. Afterward, Lee took him aside. "I'm shocked that when we were discussing material of relevance to both us, you let an hour go by without saying a word," Lee told him. "Why didn't you jump in to offer your expertise and insight? We all would have benefited." His colleague seemed genuinely surprised at the censure. "But I'm never sure I'm senior enough to say something," he told Lee.

As Lee regards this colleague highly, he was surprised that he hadn't grasped just how important it is to pivot to a more communicative style when invited into the boardroom. "Some of our businesses in Asia have been run by colleagues from outside the region," Lee observes. "That's partly because local talent has not yet gained the visibility needed to be given the role." Local talent, like his colleague, is sometimes perceived as having more technical and quantitative skills than strategic vision and as lacking the ability to build the credibility necessary to interact with divisions worldwide. Lee believes it's an unfair characterization, but concedes that sometimes he can see where the criticism originates. "There's definitely a case to be made for developing local talent to think more broadly and for equipping them with the executive presence that projects credibility to global leaders," he says. On the other hand, "there is also a strong case to be made that in order for Western leaders to become global leaders, they need to develop the cultural sensitivity to recognize forms of leadership that may be different from their own," Lee adds. Western leaders need to also master the double pivot.

Lee's story underscores just how treacherous the waters can be between the shores of local culture and headquarters—particularly with regard to demonstrating authority. Navigating these straits demands recognizing that corporate culture is its own country, reflective of, but not limited to, the leadership norms of the country (and industry sector) in which it's based. As Rosalind Hudnell, a global leader at Intel, puts it, "Corporate culture is defined by the people and norms of the organization, which continue to evolve. Our global employee base is made up of ambassadors for Intel around the world."

Our dataset affirms this divide between the West and growth-hub geographies. If we aggregate data from our US and UK samples, where most multinational firms are headquartered (certainly most of CTI's eighty-six Task Force members are headquartered in North America or Europe), a familiar array of boardroom behaviors emerges as salient. According to senior leaders in these markets ("the West"), demonstrating authority (after showing integrity) is what projects credibility.

Demonstrating emotional intelligence is at the bottom of the list.

In growth-hub markets, however, the reverse is true: when we aggregate our data from Brazil, mainland China, Hong Kong, India, Japan, Russia, Singapore, South Africa, and Turkey, we see that gravitas derives from inspiring a following and demonstrating emotional intelligence. In essence, being authoritative makes you credible with Western top brass, whereas exercising emotional intelligence is likely to earn you the trust and respect of your team in local markets.

We heard countless stories to this effect. Nicolas Japy, who runs his division out of Singapore, arrived before Sodexo's new office complex there was completed. The local manager, mortified that he had only a small room to offer to a member of the firm's executive committee, insisted that Japy take over his own office. Japy wouldn't allow it. "You're a somebody here, and others should see that when they walk into your office," he told the manager. "You've built this team, you've built this business, and it's thanks to your success that we're able to build a new facility in Singapore. When it's ready, I'll have a nice office. Until then, the small room is fine." Though it cost him some credibility with Western visitors, Japy says that in the end it won him the undying loyalty of his new team in Singapore. "You've got to show your people that if everything goes right where they're based, they have a future not just in their country, but in the company," he remarks.

GENDER MATTERS

Pivoting is further complicated by cultural expectations around gender—and by where the parent company is on the maturity curve of gender equity. In many markets (and in many corporate cultures), asserting authority and exercising emotional intelligence look very different for men and women.

Take, for example, one executive's experience running a team in Bangalore from New York. Having created a standardized approach to pricing for the firm's clients worldwide, this exec wanted his direct reports to abide by it. To ensure that they did, he created a new template. So it was with some annoyance that, during a pricing call with his Indian team, he discovered that the team hadn't complied. "Use the template," he implored the team manager. Six weeks passed, and still, the team used the old pricing model. So he called the team leader and, with the entire team on the phone, spelled out why the pricing philosophy had changed, why it would be adopted, and why he would tolerate zero deviations going forward.

He got through. In the wake of that call, the new philosophy took hold.

"Being direct, with no ambiguity, works in India; it cuts through the relatively nuanced nature of communication there," explains this executive, who's lived and worked throughout Asia. "It's a chaotic country. Everybody does things differently. To get through, to develop consistency, you have to be incredibly direct.

I made myself very clear, publicly. And now they've gotten it right."

Contrast this approach with that of Sylvia Metayer, CEO worldwide of Sodexo's Corporate Services Segment. Asserting authority in Eastern markets is not always the best way to get cooperation, she says. Metayer, who's based in France, describes a recent meeting she had with important clients in China, who were accompanied by translators. The head of the Chinese delegation opened the meeting by addressing one of Metayer's local managers, a man who barely spoke Chinese. Once the translator had finished and a response had to be given, Metayer leaped in to provide it—taking care to preface her remarks by stating that she spoke on behalf of Sodexo's board. Made suddenly aware of her seniority, the head of the Chinese delegation, who was poised to present his gift to the local manager, froze with embarrassment. "Clearly he didn't know who to give the present to," Metayer explains. To help him save face, she took her local manager by the hand so that together they might accept the client's gift. It was precisely the right gesture. "Everybody burst out laughing," she recalls. The tension dissipated, allowing the meeting to culminate in a deal satisfactory to all parties. Metayer believes that handling the situation with any less emotional intelligence on her part would have cost her team its foothold in China with this client. "The client realized he had made a big mistake forgetting that these Westerners have women who are quite senior," she explains. "My job at that moment was to prevent his mistake from becoming a business problem."

Across all markets, we find, women are consistently expected to demonstrate emotional intelligence by being aware of others' emotions, and acting accordingly—as Metayer did. For both men and women, of course, emotional intelligence is vital to projecting credibility in emerging markets, but it's interesting that EQ for women is being attuned outwardly while for men, it's being attuned inwardly. In China, for example, fully 67 percent of survey respondents thought women should be sensitive to other people's feelings in conducting business, whereas only 36 percent believed that men should. Men are expected, rather, to act in accordance with their own emotions (as 64 percent of respondents in China agree).

Gender norms similarly dictate that in many markets—Brazil, China, India, Russia, Singapore, Hong Kong, and Japan—female leaders demonstrate authority in a reserved way, whereas men are expected to flex it more assertively. In India, for example, a whopping 82 percent of our respondents thought it appropriate for men to be assertive in demonstrating their authority, whereas only 44 percent thought it appropriate for women to do the same. In Brazil, 79 percent agree that men should assert their authority, while only 46 percent believed women should do the same.

Gender matters somewhere in the practice of every single gravitas behavior. Take, for example, the imperative of demonstrating integrity, which lends credibility to men and women in all markets. How to do so varies: you can show integrity by conducting business in a way that is consistent with your *own* core values, or by conducting business in a way that is acceptable in the society where you find yourself. In China and Hong Kong, expectations of what projects integrity skew by gender. Fully 60 percent of respondents in China, and 54 percent in Hong Kong, feel that women should allow societal values to guide their business dealings; whereas 69 percent of respondents in China, and 72 percent in Hong Kong, feel that men should be guided by their own core values in any transaction.

Inspiring a following is another way for men and women to project credibility, particularly in India, China, Hong Kong, and Singapore. One can inspire a following by setting a personal example, or by articulating a compelling vision: expectations on what works best vary by culture. However, in Turkey and South Africa, expectations also vary by gender. In these countries, women leaders are expected to inspire a following by setting a personal example. Men are too, but it's more pronounced for women.

GENERATION MATTERS

Finally, pivoting among cultural norms around authority and emotional intelligence must take into account generational differences. After all, Gen X leaders can run aground of Boomer sensibilities and jeopardize credibility even when both share the same cultural background. Yet by the same token, younger leaders may have an easier time spanning vast cultural divides, as globalization continues to shrink those divides. Many of our interviewees in emerging markets point out that they and their colleagues who were born after 1980 have either completed their degrees in Western universities or worked at a multinational firm's headquarters. That experience seems to inform greater acceptance of expat talent, including women, in regions historically opposed to foreign, let alone female, workers.

For example, Karen Attyah, a director with Landor Associates, the global branding agency, recalls being pleasantly surprised at being accorded credibility by a Middle Eastern client, who ultimately hired her away from Landor to work for him as his chief marketing officer in Dubai. Part of his ready acceptance of her was attributable, she feels, to her Lebanese surname and Mediterranean appearance. Her cultural intelligence served her well ("I know not to walk up and touch a man in traditional dress"); it helped, too, that she was conversant in geopolitical affairs and attuned to religious customs. But what made all the difference, she concedes, was that her boss was under the age of forty-five, "because men his age in the UAE have all had serious exposure outside the Emirates." He had in fact been educated in Geneva before becoming a top hedge fund trader with the Abu Dhabi Investment Authority, "so he was quite modern in his approach," she explains. "He could accept pushback; he wasn't put off by my directness." Even though, in the end, she says, it was his way or the highway, "he did trust my opinion." That wasn't the case, she stresses, with his board of directors, who were a generation older. "With them, at our annual general meeting, I was persona non grata," she says. "At that age level in the Middle East, all eyes go to the Arab male in the room."

THE PIVOT PAYOFF

Rising leaders who alter their leadership style— their gravitas—as they pivot among stakeholders are rewarded for their cultural sensitivity and contextual intelligence: they are more likely to advance in their careers. Our data show that leaders who pivot well horizontally, earning the trust and respect of their team, are more likely to be satisfied with their career progression than team leaders who haven't (74 percent vs. 61 percent); that trend holds with leaders who pivot well vertically, and have won the attention and support of senior leaders: they're more likely to be satisfied with their advancement than leaders who haven't (75 percent vs. 65 percent).

Projecting credibility is a critical competency, as it earns trust and respect among various stakeholders across the divides of distance and difference. Yet it's only half the journey that emerging leaders must make to be candidates for global roles. Global leaders leverage the trust they've built to drive market success. In the next chapter, we'll look at how they do that: how they unlock value across distance and difference, and how they win the buy-in of senior stakeholders to ensure that market-worthy ideas and cost-cutting solutions get implemented.

2

Driving Value: Unlocking Ideation, Winning Endorsement

As president of Intel India, Kumud Srinivasan is tasked with more than just oversight of the chip-maker's operations in Bangalore. India is Intel's third-most important R&D site, delivering on commitments across servers, clients, PCs, and phones. To grow Intel India, Srinivasan must ensure that her subsidiary applies its talent and infrastructure to grow both the global and the local market—by innovating wherever the market is leading (for example, mobile health and transportation solutions) or coming up with ways to drive up server, PC, and tablet use. "We've achieved a solid reputation for execution," she says of her team. "The next battle is for us to go beyond that, to build our reputation as innovators."

It's a welcome challenge. Intel India is ready to move to the next level in its lifecycle of maturity. Yet it will not be easy, she acknowledges, as her team must grow their ability to influence leaders at global headquarters and collaborate better with them. "In a culture where power distance is important, it's difficult to get people to challenge decisions they disagree with, or stand their ground when challenged," she points out. Exacerbating that top-down dynamic is a seeming reluctance, among her reports, to seize the initiative. "We tend to wait to be told what to do," she observes.

But Srinivasan is shifting this dynamic. With her entire staff, she's talking up the virtues of initiative and empowerment, stressing the dangers, for the company, of their not challenging decisions they disagree with. She's created classes and workshops to strengthen not only the technical expertise of her R&D talent, but also their people-influencing skills, as brilliant ideas that fail to win buy-in will never make it to the marketplace.

Most critically, she's adopted a more inclusive approach to leadership. "I let my folks take decisions they're capable of," she says. "I explain what needs to be done, and why, but I leave it to them to strategize how." Empowering her team to lead has in turn granted Srinivasan the bandwidth she needs to grow Intel India's brand. "I'm able to focus on building strategic partnerships inside Intel, and with the government and other industry partners," she says. "Given my mandate, nothing could be more important to our success."

UNLOCKING VALUE

Successful global leaders don't just project credibility. They drive market growth. Market growth today, multinational leaders agree, depends on sustaining innovation: leaders who can unleash the innovative potential of their employees, as our 2013 research on innovation suggests, grow existing markets and crack open new ones.

How leaders do that, we find, is by creating a "speak-up culture," one in which everyone feels that his or her ideas are heard and recognized. It's vital to innovation that team members from local markets contribute their opinions and ideas, because as representatives of these markets, they're best able to identify the unmet needs of local end users. It's just as vital, our 2013 research shows, that team leaders have the Acquired Diversity® (a heightened appreciation for difference acquired from a lifetime of interacting with people unlike themselves) to be receptive to ideas they may not personally relate to, and give those ideas the backing necessary to be piloted and implemented in the marketplace. Leaders with Acquired Diversity tend to behave inclusively; and inclusive leaders, our 2013 study reveals, are more likely to create the speak-up cultures that unleash innovative potential.[32]

What makes a global leader inclusive? In our eleven-market survey, we shared a list of twenty-five effective leadership behaviors and asked respondents to indicate which ones their own team leaders exhibited. We also gauged if respondents felt they could contribute in a team setting. When we correlated the results, six leader behaviors emerged as having the highest impact on team members' inclination to contribute their ideas and opinions. In order of priority, inclusive leaders of global teams are those who:

Ask questions, listen carefully. Since early 2015, when he began working with Sodexo's executive committee as the firm's chief transformation officer, Sunil Nayak has undergone something of a transformation himself. As CEO of Sodexo India On-Site Services, Nayak knows well how to direct his reports to maximize profit and minimize loss. In his new global role, however—supporting the decision making of its executive committee as it embeds the transformation framework that will be applicable across all businesses in the more than eighty countries where Sodexo operates—command-and-control leadership has no place. "In today's world, success for any leader is about being inclusive in the way you work, and being a good influencer," he observes.

Working with a team of fifteen executives from different nationalities and cultures, he finds that success hinges on "understanding how people from backgrounds unlike your own arrive at a decision." The North Americans will make a decision quickly, and if it doesn't work out, they're happy to turn it around, he says, whereas the Latin Americans and the French will have a lot of discussion, taking in many views before making a decision—and then will want to stick with it. Understanding such differences is vital to achieving outcomes, he emphasizes. "If you impose your method, if you're not sensitive or aware of the other person's method, either you won't come to a decision or you won't get buy-in."

What this looks like in action, he explains, is listening carefully to others and asking questions to better understand their culture, their context, and their challenges. "I take my time, to find out where they're coming from, and how they want to arrive at a solution," he says. "That will shape my response. If I did not, I would lose their attention or invite disagreement."

Nayak notes that a corollary to this leadership rule is getting to know each member personally, as the way each team member responds to a challenge very much depends on his or her engagement. Discussion at lunches and dinners supports getting to know people and helps him build the trust so necessary for effective collaboration. Nayak spends the first hour having members talk about their background, sharing a bit of his own to break the ice. "They learn things about each other they hadn't known, even though they've all been working together," he observes. While such tactics might be perceived as too friendly in some cultures, and undermining of authority, Nayak feels it drives more effective collaboration precisely because it limits the hierarchy.

"Success in every part of life is nothing more than fostering relationships," Nayak concludes. "Being humble, being curious, and being a good listener all support that success."

Maintain regular contact. Isabel Gomez-Vidal, managing director and head of EMEA Sales at Moody's Analytics, meets with her nine direct reports weekly by telephone or in person and monthly by teleconference. Makiko Eda of Intel arranges biweekly one-on-one meetings with her direct reports throughout her Asia Pacific territory, checks in by phone once a week, and sends emails every day. "I reach out constantly to people not on site to collect information so I can make objective decisions," she says. "It's important to rely on not just one person, either: you need multiple inputs from reliable sources, so you can compare notes, because perceptions can be so different." Success in a global role depends on developing, quickly, a "sensor network," she says, because it's simply not feasible to travel to all the countries in her purview to gather information firsthand. Yet to develop that network, she has had to travel extensively. "Once you establish a relationship, then you can rely on that person as a sensor," she observes. "They'll pick up the phone and call me if they have a concern, or if there's something they feel I should know."

Facilitate constructive argument. Innovative ideas and bold solutions rarely emerge from polite conversation, leaders concur: what makes a brainstorm yield breakthroughs, say our interviewees, is the storm. Yet managing disruptive thinking so that it doesn't devolve into destructive argument is an enormous challenge, especially when team members are culturally diverse, or literally don't speak the same language. Global leaders confronted with this challenge consistently report that invoking a shared mission, or shared set of corporate values, keeps the argument so necessary to problem-solving constructive.

Marco Croci, VP of engineering at Cisco, describes flying from Milan, Italy, where he's based, to a Cisco corporate location to restore an acquisition whose strategic value had yet to fully actualize. Convening the firm's top leaders, the VP opened the meeting by making clear, with considerable data, that what had been a technological advantage at the time of the acquisition has been lost, over time, to the competition and how a fast moving market demands speed of execution. "It felt broken," says Croci. "There was tension." Indeed, the meeting might have devolved into finger-pointing had he not seized that moment to appeal to their professional pride, invoke their shared corporate mission, and set the conditions to operate in an open and fast-moving environment. "Let's acknowledge the challenge before us," Croci told them, "rather than spend hours analyzing why we landed here. You're all super-smart people, you're all best-in-class engineers. When things are broken, we pull together to put them right. Clear your calendars for the next three days, and let's solve this."

Give actionable feedback. This is not to be confused with issuing correctives or unvarnished criticism, says Christophe Solas, president of Sodexo's food and facilities management services—particularly in China. Clear direction is vital, especially when language barriers invite misunderstanding. Critical feedback can undermine rather than enhance individual performance, he says, as nothing is so shameful in Asian culture as making a mistake. Indeed, the oft-noted tendency of Chinese to ask no questions, raise no issues, and deliver only on what they are explicitly instructed to do is a function of this fear. "The only way to avoid making a mistake is to do exactly what you're told," Solas observes. To extract value from his team members, and encourage them to perform beyond the letter of his instruction, Solas uses feedback to build their confidence. He checks in frequently, recognizes their efforts regularly, and, when they make a mistake, offers step-by-step guidance so they understand it's not the end of the world. "Chinese people are more fragile than Westerners in their need to be reassured," says Solas. "They will thrive, perform, and deliver beyond what you ask if they feel you won't fire them or embarrass them for making a mistake, if they feel respected, and if they know they will be rewarded for their performance."

Take feedback and act on it. Isabel Gomez-Vidal used to have to travel to the Middle East quite often. Now, with a strong manager on the ground in Dubai, she only goes twice a year. "He'll tell me anything and everything," she says. It's a dramatic reversal in their professional dynamic, a product of the openness that Gomez Vidal feels she accomplished by relentlessly modeling the receptivity to feedback that she wanted him to learn.

At the outset of their working relationship, conscious of the hurdles she faced as a female leader in the region, she empowered him to be her cultural interpreter and guide. "I asked his opinion on what would work, how I might manage a difficult client conversation, what role I could take as a female in countries such as Saudi Arabia," she relates, "so that he knew I wouldn't step on his toes." By showing him that she could afford to acknowledge her limitations and be dependent on his guidance, she won his trust; by showing him she was self-aware, curious, and receptive to advice, she made it safe for him to be forthcoming and candid with her. "Now, if he makes a mistake, he'll tell me," she says. "The fact that I was open with him—that I solicited his advice and acted on it—has made him the most open member on my team."

Share credit for team success. Philippe Sachs, global head of Standard Chartered's Public Sector and Development Organizations client coverage group, tries to secure the trust of the teams he works with "in the footprint" (in Asia, Africa, and the Middle East) by ensuring they get credit for the work they do even if his teams in the various financial hubs play a high-profile role. "It's easy for bankers sitting in headquarters to get a disproportionate amount of credit for the hard work of many," he says. "It's important to give our colleagues ample profile. The more profile we give them, the more responsive they are to us, in turn."

Hence when Sachs's boss came to London for a virtual town hall, Sachs suggested he use that opportunity to call attention to the extraordinary efforts made by local staff in Sierra Leone during the Ebola outbreak and in Nepal following the devastating earthquake. "He wanted to talk about my public sector team's good work," Sachs relates. "But it was specific individuals on the ground in Nepal who came to work to make sure our branch at the UN remained operational. They may have lost loved ones, they may have been fearful of contracting Ebola, but it was the team in Sierra Leone who kept the office open. I explained to my boss that the town hall audience would include these colleagues. 'Why not give them recognition,' I said. 'You could mention them by name and congratulate the individual rather than the public sector franchise. It's going to be huge, for them, listening in on that call.'" Making his remote team members feel like equal partners, says Sachs, has culminated in dedication that redounds to the bottom line. "Our business is doing well," he says, "because teams across the world know that the value chain flows both ways."

TOP INCLUSIVE BEHAVIORS
FOR LEADERS OF GLOBAL TEAMS

We define as inclusive global leaders individuals who demonstrate at least three of these six behaviors; we define as noninclusive those who demonstrate none. We find that inclusive global leaders are far more likely than noninclusive leaders to unlock ideation: members on teams with inclusive global leaders are significantly more likely than those on teams with noninclusive leaders to feel free to express their views and opinions (89 percent vs. 19 percent), feel welcome and included (83 percent vs. 21 percent), and feel that their ideas are heard and recognized (76 percent vs. 20 percent).

Inclusive global leaders are also more likely than noninclusive global leaders to foster collaboration across cultural divides. We find that their global team members are four times as likely as global team members with noninclusive leaders to say that they embrace the input of team members whose background/expertise differs from their own (88 percent vs. 22 percent).

Finally, inclusive leaders are also more likely to foment risk-taking and disruptive thinking: their global team members are three times as likely as global team members with noninclusive leaders to say they're not afraid to fail (63 percent vs. 21 percent), and are 4.5 times as likely to report that nobody on their team is afraid to challenge the status quo or group consensus (54 percent vs. 12 percent).

This has critical implications for companies whose growth in new markets is predicated on breakthrough products and services, as a swelling body of research, including our own, suggests that leaders who don't merely tolerate failure, but rather, avidly celebrate it, unlock game-changing innovation. Since 1992, when Duke University's Sim Sitkin, professor of management and director of the Behavioral Science & Policy Center, coined the term "intelligent failure,"[33] organizations across industry sectors have sought to create cultures that encourage experimentation by stripping failure of its attendant penalties. Indeed, exceptional organizations, points out Harvard professor Amy Edmondson, "are those that go beyond detecting and analyzing failures and try to generate intelligent ones for the express purpose of learning and innovating."[34] Failing quickly and often is so much of a mantra in Silicon Valley that, as Columbia professor Rita Gunther McGrath points out, venture capitalists won't invest in a start-up unless a founder can demonstrate that he's been baptized by fire.[35] The hallmark of a failure-friendly company? A culture where employees are neither afraid to throw out risky ideas nor call attention to failure when it occurs—a culture that leaders are tasked with creating. "If an organization's employees are to help spot existing and pending failures and to learn from them," Edmondson observes, "their leaders must make it safe to speak up."[36]

WINNING BUY-IN

Unleashing ideas, spurring collaboration, and solving problems, however, is not enough: to drive value in the global marketplace and implement market-worthy innovation or cost-cutting measures, inclusive leaders must also "sell up the food chain" and garner global support. By communicating in culturally appropriate as well as gender-appropriate ways, they secure the resources and backing they need to realize their strategy for growth. While observing these nuances certainly complicates communication for emerging leaders, those who succeed are rewarded. Emerging leaders at MNCs who succeed in winning both team support and the buy-in of top executives are more likely than those lacking that support and buy-in, we find, to see their team's ideas implemented in the marketplace (64 percent vs. 57 percent).

What wins the buy-in of senior management at headquarters across markets (and, for that matter, of top executives in the US and UK) is communication skills. "Communication skills need to be refined to a higher level of sophistication," observes Paul Abbott, EVP for American Express' Global Network Partnerships business. "When you're in a global role, people will filter things you say based on the beliefs or biases they bring to the situation. So it's critical that you be very clear and concise." Abbott notes that while a spectrum of new channels has improved communication, overall, people's communication styles have become less structured, even less professional—"and that's not a good thing when you're trying to communicate across cultural and language differences. You have to be very precise, and deliberate." Abbott finds it helpful to imagine each of his interactions as caught on film. He pauses between sentences, thinking through his next words, to make them as clear as possible. "Make one mistake, and all of the good things you've accomplished are forgotten," he notes, "so focus intently on the impact of each word."

To impress senior management wherever they sit in the world, leaders must have superior speaking skills. They must also know, our data show, how to deliver a compelling message and command a room. The stakes are quite high; as Abbott observes, "If you don't set the tone right from the top, nothing will ever happen." Hence at partner meetings, board meetings, and interactions with CEOs at client firms— discussions with people who are revered in their own organizations, in the market, and in the country—he crafts his message to persuade, compel, and impress. "You're representing the brand, you're an ambassador of the company. They're making judgments about you but also about your company, your values, and your respect for others. In some of these discussions, if you don't get the blessing, the buy-in of that senior leader at that meeting, nothing happens, because these are very top-down-driven organizations."

Across all markets, in fact, superior speaking skills, delivering a compelling message, and commanding a room are communication imperatives. What differs market to market is *how* leaders should command a room, deliver a message, and speak well.

In much of the US and the UK, for example, demonstrating superior speaking skills means speaking fluent English, whereas in Hong Kong, Turkey, and Brazil it's important to be fluent in multiple languages. That learning wasn't lost on Tamara Minick-Scokalo, president of Growth Markets for Pearson, when her firm acquired the private language school business developed by Brazilian billionaire Carlos Martinez. Minick-Scokalo had taken pains to develop a relationship with the magnate, but felt it was critical to warm his franchise owners to the prospect of ownership by a big British company. So for her first meeting with franchise owners, many of whom spoke no English despite overseeing language schools, she wrote her speech, got it translated into Portuguese, and sat up all night with the head of communications, who wrote it out phonetically for Minick-Scokalo to practice. "I delivered the entire talk in Portuguese, even though I don't speak a word of it," she recalls, "and when I was done, five hundred people gave me a standing ovation." That effort, she insists, went a long way toward securing the support and cooperation of Pearson's Brazilian stakeholders, without which it would have been more difficult to implement Pearson's growth strategy in that growth hub. "It put a human face on what could have been perceived as a cold, faceless British company, after being family owned, and telegraphed our respect for their culture," she says. "It wasn't easy to do, but it more than paid off."

Our findings make clear that the way in which leaders are expected to communicate varies depending on whether they're male or female. In many markets, men are expected to deliver a compelling message by stating their conclusions directly, while women are expected to guide listeners to their conclusion. In Hong Kong, China, India, and Singapore, men are expected to command a room in a forceful manner, whereas across markets, but especially in Japan, Brazil, and Russia, women are expected to command a room by facilitating others' dialogue.

If there's a secret to prevailing in any scenario, leaders we interviewed stress this combination: integrity in message and action, flexibility in execution, and respect for others. Abbott describes traveling to Korea to deliver what he expected to be a brief speech thanking a Korean bank's executive team for its new partnership with American Express. But after meeting with the bank's CEO, Abbott was led down the hallway and through a door to confront a crowd of three hundred people, including media, waiting to hear the American Express executive's speech. "These things just happen," Abbott recalls, chuckling. "So I doubled the length of my prepared remarks. I let the translator know I was going off script. I managed to keep my manner confident and relaxed, even when I could tell the translator wasn't keeping up." Everyone left with what they came for, he says. "If you treat people with respect and dignity, take a genuine interest in them, and truly care about their success," he observes, "you can't stray too far. Those things come through in any language."

GETTING ALL VOICES HEARD

In hierarchical cultures where authority is to be respected, not questioned, is inclusive leadership anathema?

Absolutely not, say Chinese leaders we interviewed. A new generation of Asian talent that's either been schooled in the West or worked abroad embraces inclusive leadership as the key to high-performing teams. "You won't find statistics on Asian leaders enforcing a speak-up culture, but that's because it's done more subtly," says Sam Xu, head of Transaction Banking China at Standard Chartered Bank. Jenny Chan, a managing partner for Ernst & Young (EY)'s Greater China Risk Practice, agrees: with her team from mainland China, Taiwan, Hong Kong, and Singapore, she has found ways to encourage contribution without offending cultural sensibilities. "EY places top priority on inclusive leadership as a way to draw on the diversity of their people's experiences, skills, and perspectives," she says. "In different cultures, there are simply different considerations."

Here's how Xu and Chan, both based in Shanghai, have unlocked value in Asia for their firms:

Be humble. Ask questions, listen to the answers, and don't pretend to know more than you do, both Chan and Xu stress. "I'm honest about my shortcomings," Chan says. "Wherever I know I need help, I enlist people."

Invest in the relationship. Upon taking the job six months ago, Xu realized his first challenge would be to align the objectives of his branch managers with his own business objectives for the country—a communication challenge compounded by distance, as the 180 staff he oversees is spread out in three major hubs as well as branches remote from those hubs. Xu traveled extensively, meeting with managers personally to communicate his priorities for the business in the context of a slowing economy and heightened regulatory environment. It took months, but from a personal relations standpoint, he says, it was an invaluable investment. "My managers came to feel trusted and appreciated," he says. "All of my reports today feel very comfortable walking into my office to share their views and opinions."

Chan, too, is a big believer in "the journey approach," as she puts it. By taking time to get to know each of her team members personally, she has opened communication channels that make it possible for her to help them—and the entire team—solve for challenges around client service delivery as well as work/life balance. "Everyone now feels comfortable enough with me to talk openly about their career and personal goals, and ask for support to achieve them," she says. "It's made us a stronger team."

Build trust through transparency. Xu initiates a monthly sixty-minute videoconference call with all staff in all branches to update them on business performance. In addition, deal teams also share their success stories on these calls. These calls typically end with a quick self-introduction by new joiners, and a "celebration" of birthdays during that month. Six months into the job, he's reaping the benefits. "People feel more engaged, more a part of the mission," he observes, "because they know just how well they are doing both at the branch and subsidiary levels."

Ensure every team member has a voice in meetings. One of Chan's challenges upon assuming the China risk practice was getting people on her team to share their thoughts and opinions publicly, particularly the women. "I'd go to lead a meeting and the female partner wouldn't say a word," she recalls. Having grown up in Hong Kong, Chan understood that team members wished above all to avoid being disrespectful. "'Let the Big Boss say it first, I don't want to embarrass him or myself by speaking up,' is how they think," she explains. Yet having worked in the US, Chan also understood that her quieter members likely needed a confidence boost—a "pep bump," as she calls it. So she took every opportunity to make them feel competent, assuring them they were smart enough, and informed enough, to offer their opinions at meetings. She even coached her reports on how to respond if people challenged them. "If you call people out and insist they say something," she says, "you'll just make them uncomfortable. You've got to build their confidence over time."

Xu observes that the younger the team member, the easier it is to get them to speak up. "Traditionally in Chinese culture people would exchange their thoughts privately, to not embarrass the leader in front of others, but that's changing dramatically among the younger generation," he says.

Be sensitive to the importance of group support in Asian cultures. Chan's campaign to instill confidence relies, in part, on gathering the quietest voices in a safe space to support each other. At one such gathering, a female partner confided that she had not only graduated from a top Chinese financial university but also that she knew the CFO of one of the region's most significant clients. The group, amazed that this partner hadn't yet volunteered her expertise or mentioned her connections, insisted that she speak up at the next partners' meeting. "It was very comforting for her to hear it from the group," says Chan. "With that kind of encouragement, people will start to contribute ideas and values they'd never thought to contribute."

Exercise authority by holding others accountable. "My style is inclusive," says Xu, "in that I encourage everybody to share their opinions, debate them openly, and agree collectively on a way forward. But whatever targets they set, whatever next steps they agree to, I will absolutely hold them accountable."

Acknowledge unconscious bias and put safeguards in place to prevent it. To incentivize team members in Mainland China to engage in some outside-the-box thinking, Chan set up a "Best Innovation of the Year" contest.

She quickly recognized her mistake: by targeting one group, she'd inadvertently signaled to team members elsewhere that their work was less important. Since then, she's adopted two tactics to mitigate perceptions of bias and ensure everyone feels included. First, because some development opportunities cannot be extended to more than a few people at a time (a trip to Australia for a global conference, for example), Chan maintains a spreadsheet that tracks all partners and all invitations extended to date; that matrix helps ensure she allocates opportunities equitably. She also solicits the advice of another leader who's native to Shanghai. "She sees things very differently," says Chan. "Getting her perspective helps me do the right thing."

Xu likewise stresses the importance of implementing measures that prevent unconscious bias and stave off perceptions of favoritism. "When someone on my team makes a suggestion, I evaluate it based on quantifiable aspects, so as not to be prejudiced against any idea I don't personally agree with," he explains. "And if I commit to doing something based on a suggestion, I make sure I deliver on that commitment." He adds, "It's a matter of credibility, but also integrity."

BUILDING TRUST

Having lived and worked in Brazil, Canada, Chile, France, Romania, and the US, and having led operations in Eastern Europe and South America, Satya-Christophe Menard knows a thing or two about bridging the divides of difference and distance. In his nine-year tenure as CEO of On-Site Services, South America, for Sodexo, he's overseen a four-fold increase in revenues—growth that wouldn't have been possible, he stresses, had he not established close working relationships with his lieutenants on the ground.

"People won't deliver for you if they don't trust you," says Menard, who is a French citizen but grew up in South America. "You need to recognize that you must earn their trust. You cannot command it. It takes time to earn it—and you cannot command that either."

While trust-building benefits from an understanding of local culture (which Menard has, having grown up in South America), some aspects prove to be universal. Here they are:

Take time to get to know a team member in his or her own context. "You need to travel to the person, to understand his or her environment. That will allow them to show you the problems they're facing in the proper context." Offering to meet them where they sit, he adds, is especially important when they're located outside the Anglo-Saxon world. "Their perception of you will be very different if you attempt to communicate by email or videoconference," he cautions, describing how he built a global team from central Europe with people in South America. "To drive a new direction, to win their trust, I had to go meet them individually and give them the opportunity to show me who they are."

Speak their language first. Menard speaks Spanish, Portuguese, and English, as well as French. When he meets new team members on their turf, he takes a translator along. "I find it very effective because people recognize that you made the effort, and that you're being very respectful of them."

Be receptive. Make clear that you are keen to learn and open to advice. Ask questions; listen more than you talk. "Being ingenuous signals good intentions," says Menard, "and that's essential to recovering from misunderstandings."

Express yourself in culturally appropriate ways. "I try to change the form of my communication, but not the content," says Menard. "In Brazil I'm more physical, because Brazilians—both men and women—hug easily and warmly. But you cannot do that elsewhere. It would be totally misunderstood, especially by women."

Acknowledge the possibility of misunderstandings. "They are inevitable," he says. "When you acknowledge that, it releases the pressure around their consequences." Menard finds that revealing aspects of his background helps ensure others give him the benefit of the doubt, "as it explains why I might be misunderstood."

Be as clear and simple as possible about what you intend to accomplish together. Allow the other party to rephrase what you've said, to ensure you're on the same page.

"And help them see what they will get out of it," Menard adds. "People won't commit to deliver for you if they cannot see what's in it for them."

Articulate shared values and honor them. "It's imperative you establish commonality around the values of the company, regardless of the environment or culture they're in," says Menard. "Then you need to be credible and legitimate and authentic around those values. Others need to see that you're willing to put company interests above your own personal interests and values."

Avoid judging others by your own cultural references. "If you perceive in them a weakness, or suspect a wrongdoing, try to give them the benefit of the doubt," says Menard. "Believe in their good intentions; be open to the possibility that you're not in possession of all relevant information." Menard describes an incident that marked him back when he was a financial auditor for the firm and discovered an employee in Venezuela had been taking money from the company. "It turned out that a gang had kidnapped a member of her family and forced her to do it," he relates. "She was trying to save her brother. I had to fire her, but I came away realizing, it's not so easy to judge people."

While this approach to building trust has served him well over the years, Menard observes that for a global executive the process is undermined by the ever-accelerating speed of business. "We go too quickly in trying to achieve our ends in this fast-changing world," he says. "While all these communication approaches—email, text, voice, and video—make it possible to go even faster, not everyone can adjust and be nimble across all technologies. The variety of tools is much wider and yet, because we move faster and faster, mistakes get made." He adds, "For even the youngest leaders, this is going to remain a permanent challenge."

3

Mastering Virtual Communication

Six months ago, Sabrina,[37] an HR leader with thirty years of experience, left her Cleveland-based employer for a biopharmaceutical services firm that manages clinical trials, data, and medical communications for pharmaceuticals companies worldwide. While nominally headquartered in Waltham, Massachusetts, her new employer embodies the virtual management it provides its clients: Sabrina's boss operates out of Berlin, and top leaders on four continents meet weekly via TelePresence. What lured her to the firm, in fact, was the prospect of being part of its "decentralized" workforce, as she recently purchased a home in California to be nearer to her fiancé and aging mother. "The technology that enables us to recruit patients and manage clinical trials all over the world makes it easy for us to work with each other whether we're sitting in India or South Africa or Germany or the US," she says. "This company has virtual teaming baked into its DNA."

The reality, however, is far from easy. Twice a week, Sabrina is on a plane, commuting to Waltham or taking courses in Bangalore or getting to know the team in Berlin. "I'm new," she explains. "To make a good impression, I have to be present in person. I'm running the global council; I've got to go to Berlin to lead those meetings, until I've established myself."

And while she's set up in California with a suite of tools to make virtual meetings technologically seamless, she's finds it difficult to project credibility and contribute effectively even when everyone connects. Videoconferences are not very inclusive, she finds, as interacting with C-suite leaders via webcam means that she's looking at the back of everyone else's head. "It's difficult enough to be one of the few women in a meeting, but to be female *and* remote makes it especially hard to be heard," she says, adding, "We have the hardware, but not the human-ware, to make this work."

Recognizing that success in her new global role depends on her relationships with the power players, all of whom come from around the world to meet in Waltham, she's just signed a two-year lease on her apartment in Concord, Massachusetts. "To create value, increase engagement, and fulfill my mission, it's just not possible for me to work from California," she concludes. "No global leader can afford to be completely remote."

VIRTUALLY VIRTUAL

Leading remotely is a growing reality. Employees at multinational companies report that, on average, half of all communication with their team leader does not take place in person. Global executives we interviewed estimate the percentage of remote interaction to be even higher. While all of them tend to agree with Sabrina—that no global leader can afford to be completely remote, as trust is best forged in person—some foresee a day when they'll spend less time globetrotting because technology will enable a convincingly real virtual experience. "Five or ten years from now, our brains won't be able to tell the difference between real and virtual," one executive told us. "Artificial intelligence will make remote interactions more of a complete sensory experience, with touch, sight, and smell. The next generation of leaders—my kids' generation—won't get on a plane." This leader, by his own admission, is still a globetrotter. "The first visit, for me, still needs to be physical," he explains. "But technology has helped me scale that outreach significantly, and rebuild those social bonds constantly, so that instead of visiting ten members of my team in a month, I can bond with twenty-five to thirty executives in a week. I don't need constant physical presence."

Yet even as technology increasingly obviates the need to log miles equivalent, as one executive put it, "to traveling to the moon and back three times," its adoption, our interviewees agree, brings challenges. Virtual communication has introduced new ways for leaders and teams to miscommunicate, and for team members to disengage—or utterly fail to connect. And as even the most forward-looking executives will concede, seamless technology isn't yet a seamless experience for many global team participants because infrastructure varies so widely worldwide.

Our select-market survey quantifies some of the reasons why virtual meetings and brainstorms haven't yet obviated the need to hop on a plane. Fully 71 percent of respondents say that technological problems make it difficult for them to achieve their objectives when meeting virtually. Some 43 percent say that meeting virtually makes it hard for participants to read each others' emotions. Nearly half (47 percent) say that inattention is a problem. In fact, while on a conference call, 61 percent of employees admit to responding to emails, and 53 percent admit to surfing the Internet.

But in our select market sample, survey respondents and interviewees also agree that virtual is here to stay. Emerging leaders must project credibility and drive value, more often than not, via virtual channels—a reality that demands two complementary skill sets. They must acquire technical mastery of a proliferating array of virtual meeting platforms (Skype, WebEx, Google Hangout, and Blue Jeans, to name a few) as well as mobile communication applications (i.e., WhatsApp, Facebook Messenger, Viber, Google Voice) as deployed on a variety of devices (cellphones, tablets, desktop computers, and TelePresence suites). And that mastery is just the beginning. Running a virtual meeting, facilitating a virtual collaboration, leading a virtual town hall, or closing a deal with remote stakeholders requires that leaders learn virtual ways to telegraph authority, elicit ideas, invite participation, sustain engagement, and achieve consensus. As Sabrina observes, remote workers are badly in need of the "human-ware" to accompany the hardware.

To map this final frontier, we interviewed executives who traverse it daily. Cassandra Frangos, who keeps track of Cisco's senior leadership and manages a portfolio of the firm's top executives, also assembled eighteen global leaders in the US, Europe, and Asia to speak with us via TelePresence (a high-resolution video conference pioneered by Cisco that projects participants life-size to each other from TelePresence suites so that they experience each other as they would in a live setting).

We harvested from these interactions a wealth of virtual teaming tactics that in aggregate comprise the human-ware that optimizes the hardware. The next section lays out some guidance for those seeking to bridge the digital divide:

PROJECTING PRESENCE

Executives we interviewed agree: wherever the infrastructure supports it, invest in and insist on video-enabled conferencing, even if it's simply turning on web cams on employee laptops. Being able to see each other enhances everyone's ability to read each other's emotions, prevents participants from talking over each other, and minimizes members' inclination to multitask. "If you can't read facial expressions, you can't really understand why people are being quiet, necessarily," points out Russell Hoch, VP of Worldwide Service Sales strategy and planning at Cisco and a leader who believes TelePresence has transformed his firm into a truly global company. "Not that video will make you a mind reader, but with TelePresence you can see that maybe they're not understanding something." It also enables the eye contact so important to establishing credibility, says Michael Koons, VP of global systems engineering at Cisco. "If I need to understand the top five priorities you're working on," a São Paulo native in financial services told us, "it helps to look at you and hear you tell me directly while I can see your face, even by screen."

Some caveats:

✓ *Attend to your appearance.* Grooming and polish are as essential to projecting credibility virtually, leaders tell us, as they are to projecting it in person. According to fully 40 percent of our multimarket sample, looking polished wins both men and women respect and credibility; it's especially important to do so in Brazil, Russia, and the US. Nearly as many survey respondents (37 percent) say that, for both sexes, it's important to exhibit style and flair—particularly in Russia and China.

✓ *Watch your body language.* Remember, you're on camera—and on high-definition camera if you're on TelePresence. Telegraph attention: while sitting, maintain an upright posture, and keep your eyes on other participants as they contribute. Do not call attention to yourself for the wrong reasons. Refrain from eating, scratching, and other distracting gestures.

✓ *Curate your environment.* Webcams open a window onto your life. A leader in Philadelphia who "lives on TelePresence" says that she has set up her monitor conscious of the view it shares of her home office: the art on the walls, the books on the shelves, the color scheme of the room. At the very least, your environment should telegraph a degree of order and professionalism. An unmade bed in the background might make sense at 6:00 a.m. in California, but a team leader calling in from Singapore at 9:00 p.m. might infer you're unprepared, careless, or worse yet, disrespectful.

MAXIMIZING ENGAGEMENT

Nothing is more important to the success of a virtual meeting than sharing an explicit agenda and sticking to it: 46 percent of our select-market survey respondents say this ensures the team's objectives are met. With an agenda, you may engage people that might otherwise not even have planned to join the call. "I recently had a call where one member was in Australia, one member was in California, and one was on vacation, but they all made an effort despite the inconvenience to dial in for the call because they knew from the agenda that the topics being discussed were of utmost importance to them," says Ehrika Gladden, senior director of Cisco's Enterprise Services. Belgium-based Koen Bastiaens, senior director of Advanced Services at Cisco, notes that TelePresence cuts both ways: he uses it to eliminate multitasking among his team members, but their utter attention obliges him to be much more concise. "Time zones are hard to coordinate," he observes. "If I'm asking someone to join at an odd time in their day, I owe it to them to be extremely efficient. I always have an agenda and stick to it."

Other ways to optimize the time you have together by video or voice conference:

✓ *Get everyone up to speed before the meeting.* Some 32 percent of respondents say that making prereads available before the meeting in time to allow for careful reading helps ensure the team's objectives are met.

✓ *Make it easy for everyone who can't join the meeting to stay current.* Record meetings and make them available afterward (45 percent say this helps the team achieve its objectives when meeting virtually). "One of my team members is based in Antwerp now, and though *I'm* very comfortable working with her in that time zone," says Hoch, who's based in Raleigh, North Carolina, "for her, time-wise, joining us really isn't a viable option. So she records the WebEx. That allows her to go back through and listen, often while looking at the meeting notes and connecting with other members of the team to get the knowledge she needs so that she doesn't feel pressured to make all the calls as well."

✓ *Rotate responsibility for leading the meeting.* After two years of trying to elicit team contributions with limited success, a leader based in Johannesburg has a different individual assume her role and take responsibility for drafting the agenda, lining up speakers, and defining what kind of dialogue the group needs to have. "That way you start getting voices that you would not hear from otherwise," she says.

✓ *Make sure every party's concerns are accounted for and built into the agenda.* "I work with my staff to collect topics," says a manager based in Israel, "and we do a mix. I open with strategic updates for fifteen minutes, then we have different speakers. So if we finished a big launch, they will present the results; or if there's a really interesting project, teams involved have someone report out."

✓ *Write down your strategy.* "Sometimes you or members of your team will be working early in the morning, or after midnight, and you have to be on your game to make the most of that opportunity," says Hoch. "Know who you want to influence, and how best to go about it, and make notes."

✓ *Use meetings to discuss rather than present information.* Some 32 percent of select-market survey respondents say this helps the team meet its objectives. "Everyone can get the gist of a PowerPoint ahead of time," says a Singapore-based leader. "Better to use the call with everybody to zero in on key takeaways or surprise findings than walk them through the whole thing." She adds, "Just make sure you send it out in time for them to review it—and stress that you expect them to have done so prior to the meeting."

✓ *Divide teams into subgroups to brainstorm beforehand.* Face-to-face is ideal for brainstorming with a big group, but when that's not possible, gather two to three members via TelePresence. "Give them a week or two to generate ideas," says a seasoned innovator, "and then a ten-minute slot in the regular team check-in to report out their best ideas to the full group. Build those smaller teams with people who have different areas of expertise, but are on a similar level in their careers, so that they are comfortable sharing openly with each other."

FACILITATING COLLABORATION

✓ *Create a virtual social space for informal interaction before the meeting.* Ehrika Gladden opens her twice-monthly team call five minutes early and plays music. "People dial in just to laugh and talk and relax for a minute about whatever the heck I'm choosing as DJ to play that day," she says. "We've done it where the TelePresence stays open on break and people can hang out. Instead of shutting down the TelePresence, they get that time to chat with each other."

✓ *Pick up the phone.* "Just the other day, I was having an email exchange with a Dutch and Indian colleague who were having a circular written dialogue, covering the same ground over and over without understanding each other," Bastiaens told us. "I got them both to hop on the phone with me, asked a few questions a few different ways, and we got to the bottom of the issue. Sometimes, I think we are all guessing what the other parties mean on an email chain when we actually have no idea."

✓ *Create space for contribution by members from less-outspoken cultures.* "There is a risk that some cultures might fade into the background," cautions Ike Harris, VP of manufacturing operations for Cisco Asia, who's based in Hong Kong. "If you're not sensitive to cultural differences and don't create space for all to contribute in diverse ways, you won't be able to tap the full intelligence and potential of your team. The dominant culture will be the personality of the team and will yield those very typical answers that come from that particular culture."

✓ *Ask open-ended questions.* "It helps me see whether the other person understood what I'm saying," a Cisco leader stresses. "But it also provides a comfortable stage to encourage them to say what they're thinking, to confidently respond to you no matter what their cultural differences."

✓ *Adapt to the communication norms of your team.* "IM and texting do not come naturally to me," an older executive notes. "But it's the way so many of my Asian colleagues communicate, at every level of the company. When they say 'We'll talk later,' they usually mean, 'We'll IM later.' They often have three conversations going at once. I fear that it makes our conversations more shallow, but at the same time, I have to adapt and meet them where they are."

✓ *Amplify your message via social media channels.* Team members whose leaders use social media to solidify the team's commitment to their mission are more likely than those whose leaders don't to say that their leader helps maximize productivity (54 percent vs. 39 percent).

LEADING INCLUSIVELY

✓ *Rotate the time-zone in which the meeting takes place.* A sales leader we interviewed ensures that the scheduling of group calls is most convenient for the members or topics that he wants to showcase. "If I want our Asia team to be a prioritized part of our process, I time the call with them in mind; if we're discussing European initiatives and strategies, then I time the call for Europe," he explains.

✓ *Call out cultural differences early.* "When everyone is new to each other, I open our meeting by asking each team member to talk about his or her cultural background, to make everyone aware of where their colleagues are coming from, both literally and figuratively," says Bastiaens of Cisco. "Then, I try to pay attention to different ways that team members might like to engage in conversation with me, and meet them where they are comfortable. It might take a one-on-one call after our meeting, where I ask a question less directly, to get a more accurate update on their progress."

✓ *Distribute slides beforehand that communicate key talking points visually.* Close to half of our survey respondents (44 percent) subscribe to this tactic. Bastiaens makes clear why: "When not everyone on your team is fluent in the same language, you need to do more with your supporting materials to help them keep up," he observes. "Make sure you send them slides with key words in English, so that they can see what you're saying during the call and which can help them ask for clarification after the call. This is particularly important for colleagues who would fear 'losing face' by admitting during the meeting that you've lost them."

✓ *Act on visual cues.* "Just as you would face-to-face, if someone on a video call isn't speaking but looks like they might have something to say, call on them," recommends a leader based in Israel. "Curate this medium like you would a real room. Walk in early; if a colleague seems happy or sad, ask what's up."

✓ *Invite the nonpresent members to contribute first.* "It's so easy to forget the people who aren't at the table in person," says Sabrina, the HR executive who works with colleagues in Europe, India, and Africa. "Let everyone know you're interested in what they have to say but only after you've heard from your remote attendees."

✓ *Consider handicapping everyone equally.* Whenever a large group connects by telephone with many small ones, there's a tendency for those in the large group to "sidebar," or hold conversations with each other that the satellite members cannot hear, says Pascal Henssen, chief operating officer for Genpact in the Americas, Europe, and Asia. Even with videoconference, he notes, meetings confer an advantage on the home team: those who are physically present around the table can see, hear, and interact with each other far better than they can with people joining remotely. "It isn't fair," he says. "Not everyone gets the same airtime, or the same opportunity to share and defend their ideas." So back when he started working from Romania, where only eight of his fifteen leaders could join each team meeting in person, he insisted that each team member dial in from his or her own office, and not from the conference room. "I wanted everyone separated, because otherwise some of us had unfair advantages," he clarifies. "And that has become the way we work. Not only does it make remote members feel less disconnected, it's improved our effectiveness as a team."

✓ *Confer one-on-one with key stakeholders, or arrange for them to talk with each other, before the meeting.* Huge meetings by voice or video invariably break down if participants use the opportunity to iron out differences or come to an agreement on issues best discussed as subgroups. One executive working out of Singapore described the volley of calls he received before a large international meeting from people who hadn't met each other but who entertained strong opinions about each other's agenda based solely on late-night calls with intermittent connections. "One of the first things I did was to make sure key stakeholders from other parts of the world are getting clear with each other well before the big meeting," he says. Another leader based in Asia says he's learned to "precall" stakeholders so that during the videoconference he is communicating their positions, not seeking to discover them in front of everyone else. "In this part of the world, you cannot risk embarrassing people by calling them out in the meeting. Any important negotiation or consensus has to be reached privately, one on one, before the group convenes."

✓ *Structure the meeting as a debate.* Inviting pushback or discussion won't work in parts of the world where respect for authority means suppressing dissent. To encourage debate, says Ehrika Gladden, set up the meeting as just that: a debate to solve a problem. Send out a problem statement with the agenda and make clear it's going to be a TelePresence meeting. "That way they know to expect a free-for-all that allows everyone to be heard," she says. "They know that if you don't put your opinion on the table, you can't shape the final outcome. They know, because you've insisted on TelePresence, that it's important. It is critical to set it up this way so team members don't feel offended or feel like they didn't get their say, because expectations were mismanaged."

✓ *Insist everybody ask a question.* "I always do a video-conference as a roundtable; for important decisions, I get everyone to comment," says Bastiaens. "When I fear there are some misunderstandings due to cultural difference, I get everyone to ask a question. This forces the quietest members to participate, even if it is simply to say, 'No further questions.'"

OPTIMIZING IN-PERSON OPPORTUNITIES

Tech-savvy and virtually adroit leaders nonetheless recognize when a meeting or collaboration must take place in person. The majority (55 percent) in our select-market survey say first-time meetings, for example, need to be conducted face-to-face; 36 percent say it's preferable. They also recognize that it's hard to build team bonds without investing in those relationships on the ground: 51 percent of our select-market sample say it's necessary to do team-building in person. In-person meetings are also necessary to resolve conflict (according to 48 percent) and conduct performance reviews (46 percent). Millennial employees are more likely than Gen Xers to say that face-to-face is necessary for initial meetings (58 percent vs. 54 percent) and for impromptu socializing (27 percent vs. 22 percent).

✓ *Don't squander precious in-person time on the wrong content.* "We never do any readouts of anything, since you can do that on WebEx or TelePresence," says John Donovan, VP of the Global Virtual Sales organization at Cisco—a Brit who's come to master the virtual environment some three decades into his career. "The face-to-face is all about strategy debates, talent reviews—all those things where you need that intense dialogue together."

✓ *Invest heavily in face time upfront to accelerate performance gains.* When Genpact set about restructuring itself from a Gurgaon-based entity with clients worldwide to a business-operations firm with leaders in every client market, Chief Operating Officer Pascal Henssen (Americas, Europe, and Asia) was tasked with reconfiguring teams and reporting structures among four Latin American offices representing 3,500 employees. He spent the first three months meeting his new reports at all levels of the organization, face-to-face. "It was absolutely imperative that I get to know them, and show them that a leader cares," Henssen explains. "I learned a great deal about them, and they learned how things would work directly from me. I can now pick up a phone to speak with one of the hundreds of employees that I know personally. We trust one another. We know what to expect of each other, personally and professionally." It was expensive, he concedes, in terms of both time and money. Yet having led a similar transformation in Europe that took years to implement, Henssen is quite clear that this approach offers significant savings. "Because I took that time up front, we've accomplished a massive structural change incredibly rapidly," he says. "People we employ in Latin America feel this new company is a meritocracy. When everyone believes they have the same level playing field, they start delivering on the needs of the business rather than just doing their job."

✓ *Break down cultural barriers in person.* "While TelePresence is actually pretty reliable, it's so much easier to interact as a team if everybody's met once in a face-to-face environment," says Cisco's Basti-aens. With team members scattered across the US, China, Italy, Norway, Japan, the UAE, and Saudi Arabia, gathering in person is an expensive prospect. Yet with a recent project on an urgent deadline, he knew the fastest way to get everyone from storming to performing was to encourage more informal communication. So he planned a three-day event in Vienna and built in a number of ice-breaker exercises—including a game of charades. "It was very interesting to see how members from different cultures communicate," he says. "And there's no better, nonthreatening way to explore that than in a silly game."

✓ *Plan every minute of in-person time to make the investment pay off.* "I think one of the things that's changed for me as a virtual leader is that because it was easy, for decades, to meet my people face-to-face, I didn't put much thought into planning an effective meeting," says Donovan. "I kind of cobbled together some agenda items and didn't really think what impact I was trying to create. Now, I look at meetings as events. I plan out everything. I make sure the content is all aligned to what we're trying to do, that my direct staff helps take part in shaping the agenda to make sure we have the right topics in place, that we all make sure it runs smoothly in and outside of the meeting, as we're often convening in a different country." Donovan says everybody's given homework so they're ready to engage in dialogue instead of just pulling out standard slide decks for review. "From a running-the-business point of view," he concludes, "a big lesson for me has been to not be so wasteful with the time you have together."

4

Winning Sponsorship, Developing Talent

As president of American Express' consumer card business in Asia, Yat-Chung Koh is the senior-most Chinese person at the financial-services multinational. From his desk in Hong Kong, he oversees a team of direct reports in more than ten markets and is accountable for more than three hundred employees in sales, marketing, product management, and other functions. Most of his time is spent with clients in China, Indonesia, Malaysia, Hong Kong, and Singapore—but he makes bimonthly trips to New York, where top management sits. Fluent in Mandarin as well as English, and with nearly twenty-seven years of experience working for American Express across all business lines, Koh, at fifty, is keenly conscious of his career options. "Asia is going to be so important for global, US-based corporations in years to come," he observes. "Think about the importance of Indonesia, China, and the Asian Tigers: the payment business in China has outpaced that of the US. It's not like it was twenty years ago, when you might get a good salary from a Western company but have no other options. Now, I can stay at American Express at this level or go to be a CEO in a local corporation." Koh hastens to add that his blood runs American Express Blue. "The only time I'd think of leaving—and I told Ken [Chenault, chairman and CEO of American Express] this—is when I see the meritocracy is no longer happening at this firm."

Koh credits his ascent to that meritocracy. He believes his tireless work ethic, innovative thinking, and culturally attuned communication skills are what have delivered him to the top tiers of American Express' management. His leadership skills as an officer in the Singapore military helped him get recruited into the firm's satellite office in 1989, where he did "everything my boss didn't want to do;" by 1996 he was living in Hong Kong, with responsibility for human resource development throughout the Japan, Asian/Pacific, and Australia region. In 1998 the head of merchant services approached him to cross business lines and oversee merchant services for South Asia and, as he puts it, "the rest is history." Koh was promoted to general manager of China, then to CEO of the greater China and Southeast Asia card business.

Yet Koh would be the first to acknowledge the pivotal role played by individuals who believed in his potential, steered him into stretch opportunities, and advocated for his promotion at market and regional levels. From the outset of his career, he says, he attracted sponsorship, in part because he made his ambitions clear. Most importantly, however, while he was learning the business of HR in Singapore, he spent as much time as he could with the experienced executives coming through that office, both to learn from them—and to make an impression. "I listened to them talk about their objectives and plans for the coming years," he says. "I spent a lot of time watching what they were doing. I think very senior people were amazed and impressed by how interested I was in learning from them."

Koh never had "the home advantage" enjoyed by virtually all of his C-level colleagues: he never did a rotation at headquarters. But he seized every opportunity to travel to New York City, a habit he's intensified as his responsibilities have grown. "Half the time you're there because you have a global meeting, a new business proposition, or strategy for China, and you're trying to get alignment among leadership," he says. But the other 50 percent of his bimonthly travel ordeal, he says, is self-inflicted. "I want our international president aligned with the partnerships I want to do, and the people I want to work through," he clarifies.

Increasingly, in fact, Koh sees his effectiveness as a leader as dependent upon his success as a sponsor of emerging local talent. "I will put our best people in front of our senior leaders to present a new business initiative. We also have processes where I can nominate people. And I can go to my boss in New York and talk about talent because he knows all the names. There's no shortage of opportunities today for these top performers, provided they get visibility. The meritocracy works."

THE SPONSOR EFFECT

To win high-visibility roles on the international stage, emerging leaders at multinational companies need sponsors.

Extensive research CTI has conducted on sponsorship since 2010 makes clear that career progression, especially at the upper echelons of management, depends on having the support and backing of powerful advocates. Not to be confused with mentors, sponsors invest in their protégés' career success because they derive considerable benefit themselves. Effective leaders are those who form a posse of loyal and capable lieutenants, individuals who will go the extra mile to make them look good and deliver 110 percent to create value. Protégés extend their sponsors' reach in the organization, help burnish their brand, and build and secure their legacy.

In return, sponsors go out of their way to talk up their protégés, steer them into (or create) stretch opportunities or plum assignments, and defend them from attack should they stumble along the way to more senior leadership roles. They also help connect their protégés with leaders, important clients or customers, and other influencers in their professional and social circles. A sponsor will give the crucial feedback that others shy away from regarding "presentation of self," pointing out ways to improve a protégé's credibility inside and outside of the organization.

Unlike mentorship, that is, sponsorship is a two-way street. Since both parties benefit, each is incentivized to invest heavily in the other's success in the organization. The dividends that this investment pays are measurable: employees with sponsors, our 2012 research in the US and the UK reveals, are more likely than employees without one to ask for a pay raise or plum assignment, and more likely to remain engaged and be satisfied with their career progress. We find in the UK, for example, that women with sponsors are 52 percent more likely than women without sponsors to be satisfied with their rate of advancement (79 percent vs. 52 percent).[38] In the US, people of color with sponsors are 65 percent more likely than those without them to be satisfied with their rate of advancement (56 percent vs. 34 percent).[39] The "sponsor effect," in short, is significant.

WHAT IS A **GLOBAL** SPONSOR?

A SPONSOR IS A SENIOR LEADER WHO, AT A MINIMUM:

- Asks for favors on my behalf
- Advocates for my next promotion
- Supports my authority and empowers me to make decisions

AND COMES THROUGH ON AT LEAST TWO OF THE FOLLOWING FRONTS:

- Believes in my leadership potential
- Expands my perception of what I can do
- Gives honest/critical feedback on skill gaps
- Gives advice on "presentation of self"
- Provides stretch opportunities
- Provides air cover
- Makes me visible to regional leaders
- Makes me visible to top leaders at my firm
- Helps my geographic mobility

Global sponsorship, our respondents across markets affirm, works similarly but with more dramatic effect. Global sponsors ask for favors on behalf of their protégés, and advocate for their promotion. They also support their authority and empower them to make decisions—an important differentiator, one that gives rising local talent the latitude to drive value as they see fit given their market realities. In addition to these three responsibilities, global sponsors may also fast-track their protégés by making them visible to leaders regionally and at headquarters. Global sponsors can help their protégés acquire international work experience by recommending them for temporary assignments. And global sponsors can help top local talent get reassigned to new geographies (or protected from reassignment to unwelcome geographies).

The mobility that global sponsors provide translates, we believe, into greater employee engagement. Multinational employees crave exposure and experience beyond their borders: Fully 80 percent of our multimarket sample say they want to work on a team that includes people who work in other countries. Fully 68 percent say they want to live and work in another country, both in order to grow personally (say 63 percent of them) and to advance their career (say 63 percent of them). With a sponsor, they're much more likely than unsponsored colleagues to get those opportunities if asked for. Among MNC respondents in our select-market survey, 63 percent with sponsors say they've worked in another country (vs. 39 percent of their unsponsored colleagues). More than half (55 percent) who have asked for a rotation at headquarters have received it, as compared to 37 percent of their unsponsored colleagues.

As with all populations we've studied since we first began measuring the impact of sponsorship on career progression, we find that MNC employees who have sponsors are more likely than those who don't to report being satisfied with their advancement—what we call "the sponsor effect." But we also find that, for sponsored MNC talent, it very much matters where their sponsors are located. Among MNC employees with sponsors located in their local office, 68 percent say they're satisfied with their career progression (compared to 61 percent of their unsponsored colleagues). Among MNC employees with sponsors at headquarters, an astounding 83 percent are satisfied with their progression (compared to 61 percent of their unsponsored colleagues). In other words, the sponsor effect is greater for those whose sponsors work at headquarters than it is for those whose sponsors work where they work. Indeed, the sponsor effect is more than three (3.3) times greater (36 percent vs. 11 percent).

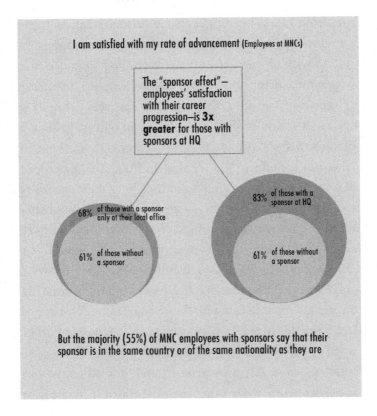

MNC EMPLOYEES GET MORE TRACTION
WITH SPONSORS AT HQ

I am satisfied with my rate of advancement (Employees at MNCs)

The "sponsor effect"—
employees' satisfaction
with their career
progression—is **3x
greater** for those with
sponsors at HQ

68% of those with a sponsor
only at their local office

83% of those with a
sponsor at HQ

61% of those without
a sponsor

61% of those without
a sponsor

But the majority (55%) of MNC employees with sponsors say that their
sponsor is in the same country or of the same nationality as they are

THE GLOBAL IMPERATIVE

Koh exemplifies the sponsor effect on talent remote
from headquarters. His gravitas and military training
won him the attention of a senior HR executive. His
devotion and willingness to go the extra mile won him
that leader's sponsorship in the form of assignment to

Hong Kong, where his solid performance attracted the leader who would entrust him with running regional teams—the stretch assignment that culminated in profit-and-loss responsibility for the firm's Asia card business. Thanks to that sponsor, Koh gained access to, and visibility with, senior management at both the regional and global level. With their support, he has won the backing necessary to see his innovative business ideas implemented in the Asia market—unlocking, in turn, a major revenue stream for American Express in the market with arguably the most growth potential in the world. Koh's ascent from a Singapore branch office to the top echelon of an international financial services firm speaks to not only the power of global sponsorship, but also to its necessity. Global sponsors build the talent pipeline that gives MNCs the competitive edge they need to prevail in growth markets.

The majority of sponsor relationships in MNCs, however, don't span the divides of distance and difference. Among our select-market sample, fully 55 percent of MNC employees with sponsors say their sponsor is located in the same country or is the same nationality as they are.

What has to change, for locals to find global sponsors? A first step would be to make sure that emerging talent understands sponsorship: what it is, why it matters, how it works—as well as how to go about earning it. Sponsorship is not owed; as our extensive sponsorship research makes clear, it must be earned. The onus is largely on the protégé to cultivate a distinctive brand, or currency, and then use that currency to attract the attention of key leaders.

David Weinert, a senior transaction manager who works in his real estate firm's São Paulo office, makes clear what that cultivation looks like. About a month into the job, Weinert perceived some communication issues between his office and New York (where the firm is headquartered) as well as with the client's team in London—issues he felt confident he could address, given his fluency in English as well as Portuguese and Spanish. He observed, for example, that his São Paulo–based client seemed grateful when he jumped in to answer questions on conference calls with London; he noticed as well that by responding to emails in a timely fashion, colleagues in New York and the client's team in London seemed grateful. But he also realized that solving these problems on telephone calls and emails wasn't going to make him visible to key people in the US and the UK.

So Weinert proposed to his local director an unusual arrangement: on his own dime, he would fly to New York and London, where he had personal business, if in turn the director would arrange for him to have desk space in both offices for the duration of his stay (and not dock him for time off). Weinert made four trips in less than nine months, during which he hardly sat at his temporary desk. "I made a point of having lunch with someone every day," he says. "I'd walk around, introduce myself, hang out in the break room. With everyone I met, I left a calling card. 'If you're in need of market information or an introduction to a broker,' I told them, 'I'm the guy in São Paulo for quick answers.'"

The strategy is paying off. A marketing director in London who puts together social events for the client globally turned to Weinert for recommendations on whom to invite from the leadership team in São Paulo. When Weinert asked his director if he could provide account coverage for a São Paulo colleague who was taking off for a month's vacation, she gave it to him, instead of handing it off to a local, "because I'd met the account director in New York at a networking happy hour and established a good rapport with him," Weinert explains. When the client's finance lead emails São Paulo looking for market information, Weinert gets copied—allowing him to provide the answers that London is seeking. "I can pick up the phone and say, 'I see you didn't get an answer, here's what you're looking for,' so it doesn't come off like I'm going out of bounds. I just have that info, to make his life easier."

Being new to the team and to the account, Weinert wants his results, above all, to speak to his value-added. But he's anticipating that by end of year, he'll be able to point to the coverage he provided on a major account and to sketch for management the role he'd like to have as a global liaison for all accounts out of São Paulo.

Weinert's story points to another crucial step for talent specialists intent on packing the global pipeline with local leader candidates: they can't afford to ignore the recommendations of middle managers who have a front-row seat on the emerging-market talent pageant.

Consider the role played by Elaine Bonner at Bloomberg LP. As global manager of Customer Account Management Support, she oversees leaders in APAC, EMEA, and AMER, with representatives in Australia, Brazil, China, Hong Kong, India, Japan, Singapore, the UK, and the US whose teams act as an internal advisory group for sales as well as operational and finance and administrative groups. Essentially, her team of leaders identifies opportunities to improve policies and procedures, thereby improving the client experience. "We learn what their needs and challenges are, and provide systemic solutions, not one-off fixes," she clarifies. As this requires a unique mix of experience, Bonner's team proactively recruits highly skilled people from each operational group: "curious, amazing people who question and challenge things, who don't care about the silos, who take ownership of the issue." Group representatives are distinguished not only by their networks ("they have people they can lean on across groups") but their passion to make things right between Bloomberg and its clients. Acting as a bridge between sales and operations, these representatives (many of whom are native to their region) gain extraordinary exposure across many different business areas, increasing their knowledge and better positioning them for future roles in the company.

Both leaders and representatives, Bonner points out, can add huge value to the company through their knowledge of the local culture and local business practices. "We have had success in each country (some small wins and some large wins) by listening to the client and identifying an opportunity to make a change that will be of no risk to the business. We then collaborate with other businesses to present our findings and discuss the value in implementing these changes. Collaborating with a global team that has diverse points of view and opinions can only strengthen our ideas." This approach culminates in a win-win, says Bonner: the client feels valued, and appreciates the agility and flexibility of Bonner's team; and her team members feel a huge sense of accomplishment. "This creates a team of people who are always on the lookout for the next big thing they can tackle," she says.

In other words, Bonner's division is sourcing, training, and engaging people worldwide whose knowledge, networks, and collaborative skills equip them to bridge silos, span cultural divides, and grow the business in critical markets for the firm.

Finally, helping local talent find sponsors with global reach may depend on connecting them to leaders who know what it's like to be "the other." Interviews with women in global roles reveal that those who've managed to communicate their value to senior leadership across the gender divide are much more

likely to be sensitive to—and committed to bridging—
the chasm that distance and difference introduce.

Joanne Hannaford, managing director at Goldman
Sachs and global cohead of Enterprise Platforms, makes
it a priority to sponsor women, especially those sitting
in offices east of New York. Having worked for the
Technology division at the firm for the past eighteen
years across many technical roles, geographical
locations, and business areas, she's keenly aware of how
her own career has benefited from the advocacy of
senior women. She observes, "I have been fortunate to
have a number of female sponsors of my career, so I try
to pay it forward to our women."

As a female partner in a division of eight thousand
people, Hannaford can testify to the value of proactively
positioning oneself for stretch assignments and high-
visibility projects. "There are significant merits to be
gained from creating opportunities rather than waiting
for them," she notes. Hence she stresses to her protégées
both in EMEA and outside the region, the necessity of
doing a better job of representing themselves and their
work to senior management. She observes, "Today,
everyone has the ability to share and gain knowledge—
success is often predicated on the effectiveness with
which we as individuals recognize and apply this." A
recurring theme throughout her years of mentoring and
sponsoring others across the globe, she says, has been
how women can best speak to their accomplishments.

"Women tend to focus first on the problems that need to be solved, rather than communicate the solutions that they are considering," she comments. "I encourage them to lead with a solution to increase their impact from the outset."

Her recent promotion to partner, she says, pays tribute to her sponsorship efforts—and to the goodwill she's developed through consistent investment in her team globally.

CASCADING SPONSORSHIP

Projecting credibility and unlocking value helps ensure that local talent gets on the radar of leaders like Hannaford. But to attract sponsorship at the highest levels, emerging leaders need to be sponsors. Seeding high-potential talent, selecting top performers for development and stretch assignments, and securing a future for them in the company beyond their own borders signals to those at headquarters that you are thinking and acting like a global leader. Indeed, as Hannaford makes clear, no one is better positioned to sponsor emerging talent than someone who has succeeded in vaulting the same barriers.

For Koh, coaching his protégés to project credibility and empowering them to drive results is immensely satisfying because the next generation of Asian talent is less burdened, he feels, by the cultural reflexes that he still struggles to overcome. They're ambitious, as he was; and they're likewise keen to live and work abroad. But they're more Westernized, as many have earned degrees in the US or UK.

They're also aware of how keenly multinational companies need them. "The new generation has very different expectations," he observes. "They won't be okay with being 'the first EVP.' They'll think, 'If I'm running our business in China, why am I at this level in the organization when the person who's running the US business is two levels above me?' They will compare themselves to the US—and it will bother them that there's a person two levels higher in the organization with a job the size of their own."

Koh encourages leaders at American Express' headquarters to intensify their sponsorship of talent in the firm's Asian footprint because, as he sees it, the pipeline in the world's hottest growth market is woefully inadequate. "Look at all the global companies: how many Asian people do they have in their top one hundred today?" he asks, and then observes, "They do not have enough people." Koh continues, "Now think about the rise of China." He lets that thought materialize before remarking, "If there aren't enough Chinese (and/or Chinese-speaking) people in senior positions, all of these companies are in for a very rough ride."

THE MAKING OF A GLOBAL EXECUTIVE

In 2007, Edzard Overbeek arrived in Tokyo to lead Cisco's business in Japan, tasked with turning the operation around in two quarters. A seasoned executive—he'd led strategic planning for Europe, and had grown Cisco's channels throughout EMEA—Overbeek was perceived as precisely the person to design and implement a strategy for growing Cisco's revenue stream in Asia's most developed market. He didn't speak Japanese, but having steered the enterprise, service-provider, public-sector, and commercial markets through challenging economic times, he'd proven he could grow market share in extreme situations. Overbeek had also impressed a top Cisco executive with his cultural fluency and (typical of Netherlands citizens) his liberal mindset. "You have a great set of attributes," the executive had told him. "Let's see what you can do in Japan."

So it was rather disconcerting, Overbeek says, to find that several weeks into his urgent assignment, his Japanese team persisted in stonewalling him. "They're looking at me, arms crossed, waiting for me to disappear," Overbeek recalls. He confided to his wife that perhaps he'd made a terrible mistake, relocating the family to Japan. "I can't see a way to turn it around," he told her. She counseled him to develop better soft skills. "You've got to listen more, talk less," she said. "Try to understand why they approach the problem the way they do."

She was absolutely right, says Overbeek: the directness that had served him well in Europe—as in, "We understand the problem, here's the solution"—was destroying his credibility in Asia. Indulging his native curiosity, he began asking more questions. Above all, he stopped believing he had all the answers. "I had to let go of thinking I knew the truth," he explains. "Truth does not exist. Our perception of reality is through a set of filters—our values, our systems of belief. Each of us will arrive, as a result of those filters, at a different conclusion which we believe is absolute truth." He adds, "Once you're comfortable with another person's point of view, and can appreciate why that person comes to it that way, then you will bond quickly."

Being keenly aware of how you come across is critical; so is a genuine interest in the other person. "You can't fake caring, people will smell it in a second," Overbeek observes. Because that authenticity test relies on so many nonverbal cues, however, he feels strongly that social bonds need to be forged in person. He invites his team up to his house, to meet his wife and kids, to see him in his home environment; he also takes team members out of the work environment to allow them to get to know each other. Authenticity bridges any cultural divide, he believes, provided that it is "packaged" in a way that's culturally nuanced.

Overbeek stresses that his success in Japan ultimately depended on forming a personal bond, and then professional relationship, with a leader who had an impressive track record in IT in Japan. The two met at a seminar and, discovering they shared a similar strategic approach, agreed to stay in touch. "He was impressed with my vision for Japan," Overbeek recalls. "He told me it would take a foreigner to turn things around, and then a Japanese leader would need to take it over in order to be less alienating to local customers and business partners." So when they met up again at a dinner, Overbeek invited the leader to join his team. "I would love to do that, but I want to run the company one day," the leader told Overbeek. Overbeek responded, "Prove yourself—after you help me prove myself." He adds, "We both perceived we could be of mutual benefit to each other in striking that careful balance of not overly Westernizing the firm's Japanese operation."

Developing local leaders and sponsoring them to rise up the ranks of the organization continues to be a priority for Overbeek. He's nurturing the careers of some two hundred high-potentials, speaking by phone or TelePresence, meeting with them in person should they come to headquarters, and mentoring them in their own offices. He maintains a circle of some fifty people, not direct reports, through whom he gathers insights on talent that wouldn't otherwise get on his radar. One of his protégés, a woman in mid-management at a call center in Mexico City, he's been coaching by TelePresence in order to help her be more effective in her market. They also talk about her career objectives and about how a move to San Jose, California, might accelerate her progress. "She has a family, so there are pros and cons," Overbeek observes. "She's concerned about the isolation, not just for her but her husband and kids. And I tell her, 'I know what that's like.'"

Yet nothing could be more important for rising leaders, he stresses, than leaping at the chance to take an international assignment. "If you want to create global leaders, let them be global," he says. "You develop skills to build relationships really fast when you get dropped into a foreign culture. You learn that people come at problems from different angles—a mindset that can be hard to embrace. But once you've had your eyes opened, to see the value that difference can bring, it's such a treat," he observes. "It's given me multiple layers of insight, and brought me my biggest rewards."

5

Global Initiatives

AMERICAN EXPRESS: ACCELERATED LEADERSHIP DEVELOPMENT

In 2011, recognizing that a changing financial and global landscape would demand a new kind of leader, American Express created the Accelerated Leadership Development (ALD) Program to arm the next generation of senior management with the critical leadership skills and competencies needed to be effective in the global marketplace.

To take part in the program, about twenty-five participants from offices around the world come together in the US for three one-week sessions over the course of six months. Development encompasses three training modules: acquiring a growth mindset, cross-cultural collaboration, and transformational leadership. Partner Duke Corporate Education leads the immersive learning experiences in these categories, which combine group work, classroom activities, and guidance from experts who address real-time business challenges. With rare exception, participants take no daytime calls or emails all week, staying completely engaged with their teammates and the task at hand. Executive sponsorship is also a key element, with senior leaders, including CEO Kenneth I. Chenault, taking on a "leader as teacher" role and joining the trainees for a portion of the program.

Lorenzo Soriano, VP and general manager of Accertify, who participated in ALD in 2012, found the curriculum to be both effective and meaningful, especially for learning about cross-cultural collaboration. The real learning, he points out, comes from spending weeks with high potential leaders from around the globe.

"When you work so closely together over so much time, you start seeing the dissimilarities in how different cultures approach certain things," he explains. "ALD provides an intimate and safe environment to learn and make mistakes; it's a place to get straightforward answers about cultural norms, like the differences between the types of bows in Japan and the reasons why someone might extend a business card instead of a hand. With this kind of training, you're spared having to learn on the job through trial and error. You walk away from the program with a basic awareness of how to navigate different cultures and with a network of people you can call any time to learn more."

Heading into its fourth year, ALD has given almost one hundred executives the training to be globally effective leaders, with more than 65 percent of participants earning promotions within two years. "ALD gives you a platform to enhance your leadership skills, which senior leaders here recognize," says Mayra Garcia, VP of executive talent development. "Once you're in the program, you're part of a highly visible talent pool."

In fact, just one year after ALD, Soriano found himself relocating to Chicago from Mexico to take the helm of Accertify, the fraud prevention vendor that American Express acquired. "ALD has proven invaluable, not just in preparing me for a global role, but in connecting me to key leaders, as many of my ALD classmates are managing entire divisions now," he observes. "When you're suddenly faced with global responsibilities, nothing is more valuable than being able to pick up the phone and have a direct line to the leaders who can mobilize the resources you need."

BLOOMBERG: GLOBAL CALL IMPACT

Global calls are becoming an increasingly common part of the work day, yet many face challenges working across distance. Politely interrupting a colleague, addressing multiple people, or getting a point across clearly are simply more difficult over the phone. At Bloomberg, about 20 percent of managers now have team members in an office or region different than their own. Because of the obstacles accompanying this trend, Bloomberg's leaders joined forces with the Tokyo-based AMT Group to create the Global Call Impact program in 2011. It's a three-hour workshop that helps employees identify their own unique points of pain on international work calls. Since then, the program has helped hundreds find their voices in the now-commonplace, yet still difficult to navigate, global conference call.

Global Call Impact is rooted in the understanding that while global calling has become a fundamental aspect of conducting international business, it requires effective leadership and confident contribution—qualities that don't come naturally in a virtual meeting spanning multiple time zones. The three-hour program first focuses on typical barriers to speaking up and the consequences of not doing so, with facilitators working with each individual to identify his or her reasons for staying quiet. Facilitators then give participants feedback and practice through three conference call simulations with up to twelve participants—the intimacy of such a small group ensures all participants receive nuanced advice. In the debriefings that follow each simulation, facilitators identify what held each individual back from effectively contributing to the meeting and offer tips to help them improve in the next round.

"Everyone walks away with something practical to try," explains Rebecca Midura of the Leadership Learning and Organizational Development group at Bloomberg. "It's unique because it isn't about time or meeting management; it's focused and actionable." To ensure that they put their learnings into practice, participants go back to their managers and seek feedback on two specific actions they will take on future conference calls.

According to Midura, similar problems persist in videoconferencing, so it remains imperative to be effective on a global call. She notes that call leaders are the most important audience to reach with this program and, unsurprisingly, the most difficult group to get into training. "To get call leaders as involved as call participants, this should become a part of their communication training," she explains, hoping to identify and pull in leaders who are effective in person but fail to fully convey their skills over the phone.

More than five hundred people have gone through Global Call Impact. A participant satisfaction survey shows participants find the program effective and relevant, and are likely to recommend it to peers. Facilitators of the program are most gratified, though, by the "lightbulb moments" witnessed during the simulations. For some, it's hearing familiar feedback from the facilitator and finally having it sink in; for others, it comes naturally with having someone observe them on a call for the first time. "It's been really rewarding to see people identify something standing in the way, and then walk out of a session saying 'I can try this next time I'm on a call,'" Midura says.

CISCO: BUSINESS LEADER FORUM AND HIGH POTENTIAL SENIOR DIRECTORS PROGRAM

In 2011, as Cisco began to transition from hardware manufacturer to solutions-and-services provider, its executive talent team sought ways to have future leaders help shape the evolution of the company. Although Cisco's reputation for technological advancement makes continuous change seem like business-as-usual, with seventy thousand employees it's remarkable that radical innovation consistently makes it all the way to market. The Business Leader Forum (BLF) and High Potential Senior Directors program are two initiatives that facilitate this innovation and the diverse leadership that make Cisco a game-changing firm.

The Business Leader Forum brings together a different twenty to twenty-eight person cohort of Cisco's top executives from around the world two or three times a year. The three-day program begins with a big-picture view: executives have an opportunity to hear about Cisco's strategy directly from C-suite leaders. Then, they form cross-functional teams, receive leadership assessments, and work together to solve high priority strategic problems chosen directly by the C-suite. At the end of three days, participants present their solutions to the organization's operating committee, which consists of the top ten people in each company function.

While BLF began as a way to have Cisco's highest potential top executives engaged with the C-suite working on critical business issues, it has evolved into a program for integrating those who have just joined the executive ranks after recent promotions, hires, and acquisitions. "BLF offers the perfect platform for teaching the broader Cisco strategy to new executives," says Cassandra Frangos, VP of global executive talent, workforce planning, and organizational development.

BLF has been integral in driving cross-functional business relationships. "New VPs, especially those coming through acquisitions, are so glad to have the chance to find others at their level operating in different functions or countries who are faced with similar challenges," notes Frangos. Such global alignment ensures an unhindered pipeline for innovation and exchange of ideas.

High Potential Senior Directors is a separate program that takes the principles of BLF and targets the next generation of leaders who are on their way to VP roles. The intensive, ten-week-long program pulls together thirty high-potential leaders and, in cross-functional teams, has them draw on one another's expertise to develop innovative solutions to strategic problems set forth by a sponsoring SVP. They accomplish this by working virtually, using Cisco technology to collaborate with one another across geographies and time zones; over the course of three virtual meetings, sponsors give participants one-on-one assessments of their strengths and developmental needs. "They go about their day-to-day work with others in their division and then suddenly have to communicate with a team of people who think so differently," elaborates Frangos. "But as a result of that interaction, the sponsor gets this new strategic view and synthesis of the problem they're trying to solve—not just the data output that they're accustomed to seeing."

A good number of participants have been promoted to VP, says Frangos, and several have gone on to participate in BLF. The High Potential Senior Director program gives the top executive team a window on the organization's future executive leaders, and at this point has enough alumni, Frangos notes, to enable it to function as an ongoing community of peers that are engaged in each other's development as well as in driving Cisco's transformation. Participants leave the program deeply and notably attuned to the future needs of the business. "They realize how their work contributes to our longer-term strategy," observes Frangos. "The most rewarding part has been watching these executives develop, make a business impact, and envision a clear career path for themselves at Cisco."

EY: MENA CULTURAL INTELLIGENCE STRATEGY

Intent on winning the business of a major industry player in the Middle East, an EY member firm partner who had lived and worked in the UK for forty years arranged to meet his prospective client in their offices in Dubai. He envisioned the meeting as an opportunity to demonstrate his technical skills and convince the client of his team's expertise. Upon his arrival, however, he found himself meeting not with the client but rather, with his senior management. Not until the end of the meeting was he formally introduced to the client. The partner was welcomed to the region and to the country by the client and a short, high-level chat took place without going into any details of the project at hand. The client shook the partner's hand and said, "The management has vouched for you and recommended your service, so we will do business."

The meeting, and its outcome, took the partner by surprise. "So much time went into the planning and preparation for this meeting and I barely got to speak with the client. I did not even have the opportunity to show how I could add value to the client's organization," he told his team.

Experiences like these are why EY created and adopted its comprehensive Cultural Intelligence Strategy in MENA (Middle East/North Africa). Some of the GCC (Gulf Cooperation Council) countries comprise large expatriate populations; in some metropolitan cities, expatriates outnumber citizens. With employees representing more than seventy-five nationalities, EY is aware of the need for its leaders working in MENA to have the tools to navigate the divides of cultural difference.

The journey of developing EY's cross-cultural competence program in MENA started about four years ago with the establishment of a MENA-wide diversity and inclusion (D&I) strategy. The MENA D&I team worked with an external consultant to design a Cultural Intelligence Workshop that has since become mandatory for all EY employees working in MENA, regardless of rank or role. They also designed simulations of scenarios that employees might encounter in the

Middle East in order to train them on how to proceed in the face of uncertainty and ambiguity. "You can't talk about cultural intelligence without talking about someone's beliefs, norms, values, and religion," observes Hasan Rafiq, assistant director of D&I in MENA. "So we have to bring these sensitive topics to the table and determine how they drive behavior."

For instance, Rafiq explains, people foreign to MENA fail to understand that business in the Middle East doesn't usually happen without credible referrals based on strong relationships. "It's about community, not individual accountability," says Rafiq, who was born and raised in Pakistan.

When teams return from client interactions with new issues and challenges, the MENA D&I team takes this anecdotal experience and, after supplementing it with outside consultation and research, creates a module to coach future teams. Tailored sessions are also created to coach partners newly assigned to the region.

Commenting on the value and impact of this learning, Yasmeen Muhtaseb, advisory partner of EY Jordan and MENA leader of D&I, says, "At EY MENA we're growing increasingly capable of preparing people to handle whatever challenges they come across. From a business standpoint, there is enormous value in fully enabling all our partners and business leaders to work effectively in a crosscultural environment. This has been proven to bring further success and growth of the EY brand."

EY: GLOBAL NEW HORIZONS

In 2008, EY took a new approach to improving collaboration and communication across country borders. "Increasingly, a basic understanding of other countries was not enough," observes Paul Hardoin, associate director, human resources at EY. "We needed something strategic to really get people in connected regions working together more effectively." The result was Global New Horizons, a three-month international rotation program that gives high-potential employees the chance to work on global client accounts earlier in their careers, develop robust networks, and immerse themselves in new cultures. The program, which began in the EMEIA area and quickly spread to the Americas and Asia Pacific areas, now facilitates placements worldwide.

The priority is to give participants from mature markets an experience in an emerging market and vice versa, such as a move from the US to Brazil or from Singapore to Australia. Program leaders work with the service lines to choose high-performing applicants who have established they want a long-term career with EY and can present a strong business case for an international experience. Participants have sponsoring partners on both ends with whom they draw up an assignment plan to define objectives for their time abroad, detail the expectations for what they'll contribute to their new team, and identify the skills they'll bring back to their home office. To date, over one thousand employees have participated in the program worldwide; 72 percent have gone on to work on one of EY's key global client accounts.

"Global New Horizons has provided strong performers from countries like Zimbabwe, Turkey, or Vietnam with a unique international experience," says Susanne Seefeldt, EMEIA program leader. "This provides real long-term value to the home country and is also a great example to graduates of how global EY really is."

The whole premise of the program, elaborates Claudia Subirat, Asia-Pacific mobility program manager, is developing a global mindset—and network. "We want people working across borders, establishing those international connections that will become invaluable in their career progression at EY," she says. Through social media, cultural orientations, and online cultural tools, participants are able to prepare for their experience and connect with each other. In the Americas area, all participants coming to the US meet in person for two days and complete a cultural orientation before going out to their new locations. "Even after two days they get very close," observes Hardoin, who directs Global New Horizons in the Americas. "Between this camaraderie and the three-month experience, the network becomes one of the biggest benefits they achieve."

Participants attest to the program's benefits. "It has been the best professional experience in my life so far," wrote a Chilean on rotation in the US. A participant on rotation in India from the UK wrote, "Global New Horizons had a profound effect on me personally and professionally. Working as part of a new innovative team in India pushed me to think further outside the box. I learned so much about the culture and much about myself in the process."

With interest in Global New Horizons increasing exponentially—the number of applications far exceeds the number of available spaces—some business areas have started to put forward the funding out of their own budgets to ensure additional candidates from their divisions are added to the next cohort. "It's wonderful that they see the value in having their people go through this program," notes Subirat. "With the businesses themselves taking a greater interest, it's clear that the program will only continue to grow."

GENPACT: INTEGRATION FRAMEWORK

In recent years, Genpact has hired a large number of VPs from outside of the company. Most of these hires are client-facing and may come from hierarchical corporate cultures very dissimilar to that of Genpact. "It became paramount for us to buff up the integration program and fine-tune it to the needs of our new employees," says Mathieu Oudot, HR leader for sales. "Their potential impact on us is invaluable, but they need to feel comfortable here to make that impact." For Genpact, this meant revamping its framework for integrating new leaders and familiarizing them with the organization's culture and global mindset as efficiently and effectively as possible.

The framework has several components. First, new VPs draw up a one-hundred-day plan in collaboration with their supervisor, incorporating as many opportunities as possible to train and network, and tweak it over time to match their interests and preferences. Additionally, new VPs are given a buddy: someone who shares his or her network, offers growth opportunities and exposure, and provides a safe space for asking questions and learning about Genpact's culture. Buddies are often more senior, but not in the VP's direct chain of command, and they tend to be selected based on their own integration within Genpact and reputation for honest feedback.

A crucial component of the integration framework is the Global Integration Workshop, which brings together the new leaders for a full week in one of Genpact's Gurgaon, India offices. Part of the week is dedicated to teaching Genpact's strategy and giving the VPs the opportunity to meet with and learn from board members and the CEO. The remainder of the week focuses on familiarizing the new hires with Genpact's product offerings—with visits to local sites to better understand the company's operations—and on networking dinners, featuring key company senior leaders.

Back in their local offices, the newly minted VPs also meet with their assigned HR professionals each quarter to provide feedback about the program and voice any challenges that HR can address with their managers. They also attend monthly virtual presentations run by the CEO's direct reports who "speed-coach" them on a relevant skill and engage everyone in discussion afterward.

Program leaders measure the integration framework's success by the rate of retention in the first twelve months (99.2 percent in 2014) and rate of satisfaction (98 percent in 2014). A new-hire survey, administered three months into joining the organization, garners this information as well as valuable feedback on how new hires are progressing and how at home they feel within Genpact. "The satisfaction scores of the newcomers are just amazing," says Oudot. "They feel like a part of the organization, and as they move on to become supervisors, they are much more rigorous in implementing this integration."

As it develops, the integration program continues to incorporate more activities and become more granular in addressing individual needs. Oudot remarks that a one-size-fits-all approach diminishes each individual employee's unique contribution to the organization, and that it is just as important for the new hires to bring their own influence to Genpact as it is for them to fit in.

"We don't hire these leaders just hoping that they'll comply with our structure," he explains. "We want them to integrate, but also to influence us; they are senior enough to make that happen." In this way, new leaders can quickly find their place and their voice within

Genpact, leveraging their diverse global experiences to create growth and positive change.

GOLDMAN SACHS: CROSS-CULTURAL PROGRAM

As a firm seeking commercial opportunities around the world, Goldman Sachs recognizes the importance of collaborating globally and empowering local employees. Yet, operating a global business doesn't come without its complexities as diverse geographies, languages and cultures integrate.

Culture is complicated. It is something learned over time that transcends birthplace and ethnic background. Culture shapes our behaviors, preferences, and style. A person's cultural values could manifest in deeply held beliefs about what is right, appropriate, and acceptable, and what isn't. For many employees, navigating cultural differences and overcoming cultural norms is important to work effectively in a global organization.

To address this, in 2009 the firm developed the Cross-Cultural Program to help employees better understand cultures apart from their own, navigate these differences, and shape improved outcomes. According to Jen Moyer, managing director in the Human Capital Management division, "As our business grows, our talent is more diverse and globally dispersed; having the ability to flex one's style and be culturally competent while still being authentic is an essential leadership behavior, not just a 'nice-to-have.'"

Launched in Japan and other key Asian markets, the programs target employees whose roles are starting to expand beyond their home offices. Using the insights of senior leaders who had already effectively flexed their styles and bridged cultural gaps, the program consists of five one and a half–hour training modules that explore critical cultural challenges and offer tactical ways of addressing each one. For example, one module called "The Art of Escalation" explores the differences in approach to handling a problem: whereas culturally in Japan it is usually the individual's responsibility to fix it, at Goldman, it is imperative for individuals to alert everyone ("escalate") and have as many hands on deck as soon as possible. Other training modules focus on executive presence, being seen, and applying a variety of communication channels. The opening module introduces a tool called GlobeSmart, made available through Aperian Global, that gives participants a point of reference for their cultural preferences by comparing them on five dimensions: independent vs. dependent, egalitarianism vs. status, risk vs. certainty, direct vs. indirect, and task vs. relationship. Each module includes a senior leader speaker sharing best practices and developmental exercises—such as performing an "elevator speech"—to put into practice the key learnings.

The Cross-Cultural Program expanded within a year of its pilot in Japan to Korea and then India, Singapore, and Brazil. Most recently, customized versions of the programs are also being piloted in Hong Kong and China.

Each region tailors the program's thematic content; for example, the Korean office has a module focusing on networking, and the Singapore program includes a module on "elevating your personal brand."

Sherry Greenfield, VP and head of Goldman Sachs University Japan, observes how powerful it is to bring these cultural disconnects to light. "At each kick-off event," she explains, "participants come to realize that what appear to be their own personal issues or unique experiences are in fact problems shared by many in their office and region—and they can overcome them."

Before and after each five-month program, participants and managers are surveyed to gauge, in qualitative measures, the impact of the program in terms of behavioral change. Overall, participants feel the initiative has been highly successful. In one example, a participant realized the power of using a variety of communication channels when he received an immediate response to a voicemail inquiry, having failed after many attempts to elicit a response over email. "They definitely feel more effective," observes Greenfield. "These programs clearly address a key developmental need among our most promising emerging leaders."

GOLDMAN SACHS: PINE STREET'S GROWTH MARKETS NEXT GENERATION PROGRAM

In 2014, recognizing the need to further invest in and strengthen the leadership pipeline of Goldman Sachs' growth markets offices, the Pine Street leadership development group designed and delivered a new program for a select group of high-performing VPs. The objective of the program was to provide participants with a unique experience that helped them build and deepen relationships with senior leaders across the organization, better understand the firm's business strategy and risk-management approach, and enhance their leadership and people management skills.

To achieve this goal, Pine Street generated a new idea: bring these emerging leaders to corporate headquarters in New York for an intense four-week program and immerse them in the firm's culture and day-to-day operations. "We wanted to give them real visibility with senior management and we knew it had to be about much more than just casually meeting one another—these interactions had to center around specific business discussions and opportunities," explains Katie Dowbiggin, a Pine Street VP. Working closely with divisional and regional leaders from around the globe, Pine Street identified thirteen VPs from six countries to participate in the inaugural Growth Markets Next Generation program.

Throughout the program, participants attended and led round-table discussions with senior leaders, heard from divisional leadership on the state of the firm's businesses, including businesses of which they were not members, and observed important firmwide committee meetings. Another important part of the program was giving participants the opportunity to learn how significant cross-divisional deals had been executed within the firm. Senior leaders responsible for different deals met with the participants and shared their experiences in delivering complex and commercially-successful projects. The VPs also participated in a number of networking events as well as skills sessions taught by executive coaches on topics that included communicating effectively, leading with presence, and influencing stakeholders. The rest of their time was spent engaging in specific divisional activities including work shadowing, internal consulting projects, and presenting to divisional committees about their growth markets.

For additional support, integration, and counsel, each participant was assigned a sponsor to oversee his or her career development. The VPs were also paired with a peer buddy in the same division to help them build their professional network, and ensure they had a positive and meaningful experience while in the New York office.

The participants returned to their local offices eager to share their learnings and observations from the four-week program. Initial feedback from the program's first cohort has been very positive and a number of senior leaders have indicated they've already observed an immediate change in the program participants. "Their network grew immensely and we fully expect to see ongoing benefits," elaborates Dowbiggin.

"The Next Generation Program has instilled in these future leaders a passion for advancing the firm's business principles in their local markets," says Nicole Grozinski, VP of Goldman Sachs University. "Throughout the program, they established a strong connection with one another and now have a network of peers that extends well beyond their local office. The participants feel motivated and empowered in a way they didn't before."

INTEL INDIA: PROTÉGÉ SPONSORSHIP PROGRAM

To give more global exposure and developmental opportunities to its pipeline of female VPs in India, Intel launched a formal sponsorship program in 2013. The India Protégé program's first cohort includes an elite group of eight senior engineering managers paired with worldwide sponsors who are one or two levels above them (yet operate outside of their chain of management) and share similar interests. "Having a sponsor in Hong Kong or in the US," explains Vasantha Erraguntla, director of Technology Pathfinding at Intel, "gives each protégé a global perspective, otherwise impossible to attain, as well as an understanding of other business areas, which is crucial for obtaining a more senior leadership role."

Sponsors are required to take an active role providing advocacy, not mentorship, to ensure real growth opportunities. They share their local networks with their protégés and meet with them in person whenever traveling in that region. Sponsors and protégés are responsible for setting the parameters of their relationship, and they meet virtually at least once every two months.

Whenever a senior sponsor executive is on-site, program facilitators bring that executive and all eight protégés together in an informal setting for a no-holds-barred conversation. "This offers a truly rare networking opportunity," notes Erraguntla, "one whose power is evident in how often the protégés and executives reach out to one another later."

Additionally, the women attend a workshop to ensure they leverage their sponsors and networks for additional visibility. "We tell them their aspirations are paramount and it's okay to ask for what you want," elaborates Erraguntla. "Just mentioning that they're a part of this program has created a lot of opportunities for them to go knock on doors they were otherwise hesitant to. They say, 'I'm a part of the India sponsorship program,' and right away that person knows they're hungry and ready to take on new challenges."

The program has already culminated in considerable mobility for these protégés. Six of the original eight participants have expanded their scope of responsibility; two have seen direct promotions, and another protégé has moved to the US. Most have maintained close relationships with their sponsors. A second cohort is now cycling through the fifteen-month program.

Erraguntla and her colleagues encourage program alumna to sponsor junior women or give them leadership opportunities; to consider, for example, assigning a project lead to a high-potential woman who may not have had the opportunity to prove herself yet. "In this way, without sacrificing the many benefits of keeping the cohort small, the program can continue to generate impact," says Erraguntla.

PEARSON: EMPLOYEE VALUE PROPOSITION

As a global education company, Pearson has an inspiring mandate to serve the students and educators using its products. The company wanted that mandate to become an even greater source of pride and motivation for its employees. The company had strong legacy values that were used as a touchstone around the world but with an enhanced ambition in education, wanted to test the relevance and role of those values for the future. The goal was to bring those values to the forefront and build them more explicitly into everyday behavior and decision making.

Together with Hewlett Consulting Partners, Pearson sought to connect with employees and test the values and behaviors they wanted to see defining the company's trajectory. The first step: gauge their connection to and engagement with the Pearson mission (improving learners' lives through learning) and Pearson's core values (brave, decent, and imaginative). Through a series of interviews and virtual focus groups, Pearson learned that their employees feel a strong connection to the Pearson mission and are willing to go the extra mile to help achieve it. Further, they feel Pearson's values make the firm unique from other employers and seek to strengthen these values with a greater focus on collaboration and transparency.

With this better understanding of its workforce's outlook, Pearson leadership added "accountability" as a fourth core company value. Giving employees an even greater voice, the values were talked about at the annual Global Leadership Conference, attended by 150 leaders and streamed to all employees around the world. This was an important step in promoting the culture that will drive Pearson's purpose to make a measurable difference to learners' lives.

Further, through an improved learning environment and greater clarity on the diverse range of career opportunities available, Pearson hopes to create the conditions that enable 'learning for all, everyday' so that everyone within Pearson, regardless of geography, age, or gender, has the opportunity to grow professionally and personally.

PFIZER: TALENT MARKETPLACE

In 2014, as part of a leadership development program, a cross-functional, cross-cultural team of Pfizer employees tasked themselves with solving a thorny organizational issue: how best to facilitate greater mobility across Pfizer business units, help employees develop, and prepare employees for future roles. The solution, which they presented to senior leaders at the close of their program, was a global job exchange accessible through the company's intranet. The online forum would allow any colleague to post or apply for short-term developmental opportunities within Pfizer, ranging from joining a team in a different division for a three-month project to shadowing a senior leader for a day.

Impressed, senior leaders green-lighted the initiative for development, and in June 2014, Talent Marketplace went live. "It's colorful, intuitive, and easy to use," says Connie Bustamante, director of career mobility in Worldwide Talent and Organization Capability at Pfizer. Those in need of a project manager, for example, can post a description of the project, the site, the skills or experience they're looking for, and the duration of the engagement. Selecting candidates is up to the person who makes the posting. Depending on the scope of the engagement, individuals can decide to formally interview candidates or simply connect via email.

Employees may commit up to 30 percent of their time to these extracurricular opportunities, says Bustamante, approximately 25 percent of which take place entirely virtually. About half of the Marketplace's four hundred participants seek opportunities within their business areas, she says, while the other half seek opportunities outside. "This gives Pfizer a unique edge in the battle to foster internal mobility and development, given that, as research shows, it improves employee engagement and has a significant impact on business results," she explains. "If colleagues are able to develop their skills within their organization or explore roles outside of their team, the opportunity to create their own change is now at their fingertips. Talent Marketplace breaks the cycle that happens when you really want to advance your career path but are denied the opportunity to gain experience on the simple grounds that you *have* no experience in the function you are interested in pursuing."

Talent Marketplace doesn't just open doors for employees; it brings project teams and leaders invaluable new perspectives and problem-solving approaches. Many teams can benefit, Bustamante notes, from the insights of someone from another division who has an intrinsic motivation to learn about and develop new skills within a different business unit. This symbiotic relationship between program sponsor and employee sets Talent Marketplace apart from standard development programs, ensuring that opportunities are offered and sought out automatically—"no planning, expenditure, or pressure is necessary," Bustamante points out. Sponsors, she adds, are enthusiastic about creatively leveraging the tool to fill gaps for diverse business needs and situations.

As of July 2015, Talent Marketplace has been translated into eight languages and incorporates email alerts, which give participants instant notification when opportunities that meet their preconfigured criteria arise. These changes are the direct result of feedback from a survey built into the site; Bustamante anticipates Talent Marketplace will continue to grow and better serve those who use it based on this feature. "It's a truly inclusive development tool," she says. "It doesn't just target people at a certain level; it gives everyone at Pfizer the opportunity to grow and control their own career trajectory."

SODEXO: GLOBAL AGILITY

To reinforce its transformation from a geographically segmented international company to a truly global organization, Sodexo has implemented Global Agility, a series of initiatives and training modules designed to promote cross-cultural competence and connect business units and leaders in its 32,700 sites worldwide.

Some parts of the initiative are still in the planning phase, while others are in full swing. The first step has been regional kick-off meetings, currently occurring in twelve regions but soon to expand to more, to show executives why adopting a global mindset is mission-critical. Using the Cultural Orientations Indicator, part of a suite of tools and training offered through Cultural Navigator®, executives can learn about themselves and others in terms of their preferred styles of thinking, interacting, and problem-solving in work-related situations. These sessions serve as a point of departure, helping executives identify the cultures in which they would function best and understand how to shift their interactions when operating in less-familiar environments to be able to connect meaningfully with others.

Phase Two of the initiative will disseminate this mindset shift to other senior leaders with a half-day training module, and will focus on skill building in leading virtual global teams, building trust across cultures, and giving feedback and providing recognition—all critical skills for building high-performing global teams. These modules will provide resources and learning beyond the inclusion training Sodexo already mandates for managers.

Additionally, a resource center on "Global Mindset/Cultural Agility" will become available through the company intranet for all managers, providing tools that will support them in leading globally. "The idea is a one-stop shop for anyone needing these insights," explains Jodi Davidson, director of diversity and inclusion initiatives at Sodexo. Resources in a range of formats will cover topics such as managing global virtual teams, maximizing cross-cultural collaboration and communication, leading flexibly, and engaging local top talent.

Sodexo hopes to expand a mentoring program currently in place to pair more high-potential individuals with leaders in countries other than their own. This gives emerging leaders the perspective and experience they need for international mobility, explains Satu Heschung, director of global diversity initiatives.

As more efforts fall under the umbrella of this initiative, program directors anticipate that Sodexo's leadership will reflexively think globally and manage cross-culturally. That's important, says Heschung, because Sodexo's clients are looking to Sodexo to help them with their own transition to global operations. But there's another benefit, one with far-reaching implications for the firm in terms of securing the best talent and keeping it: executives with a global mindset tend to be more inclusive leaders. "All our partners and team members are diverse in such valuable ways," observes Heschung. "The inclusivity created by a global mindset helps us capitalize on the abilities of all of them."

ENDNOTES

1. Judith Elliott, ProPublica, and Laura Sullivan, NPR, "How the Red Cross Raised Half a Billion Dollars for Haiti and Built Six Homes," ProPublica and NPR, June 3, 2015, https://www.propublica.org /article/how-the-red-cross-raised-half-a-billion-dollars-for-haiti -and-built-6-homes.

2. "Humanitarian Assistance, Emergency Relief, Rehabilitation, Recovery and Reconstruction in Response to the Humanitarian Emergency in Haiti, Including the Devastating Effects of the Earthquake," United Nations General Assembly, September 2, 2011, http://reliefweb.int/sites/reliefweb.int/files/resources /RSG_A -66-332_EN.pdf.

3. Elliot and Sullivan, "Red Cross" (see note 1).

4. While trade to emerging markets is expected to continue to increase, rising to upward of 47 percent of global consumption by 2025, McKinsey estimates that the number of large companies based in emerging regions is also set to more than triple—soaring from 27 percent to 45 percent of the global total today. Based on projected growth by region, these emerging companies will account for more than 45 percent of the Fortune Global 500 by 2025. Correspondingly, the number of Fortune Global 500 companies headquartered in developed countries will fall from 75 percent to less than 55 percent by 2025. (McKinsey Global Institute, "Urban World: The Shifting Global Business Landscape," McKinsey & Company, October 2013; Jacques Bughin, Susan Lund, and James Manyika, "Harnessing the Power of Shifting Global Flows," *McKinsey Quarterly,* February 2015.)

5. A vast body of literature concerns the positive impact local talent can have in aiding MNCs in navigating new and emerging market dynamics, including notably P. Rosenzweig and H. Singh, "Organizational Environments and the Multinational Enterprise," *Academy of Management Review* 16, no. 2 (April 1991); Y. Gong, "Subsidiary Staffing in Multinational Enterprises: Agency, Resources and Performance," *Academy of Management Journal* 46, no. 6 (December 2003); and G. Frynas, K. Mellahi, and A. Pigman, "First Mover Advantage and Multinationals Firm- Specific Political Resources," *Strategic Management Journal* 27, no. 4 (January 2006).

6. Local talent from emerging markets are much more likely to exhibit both inherent and acquired diversity, such as diverse gender, race, ethnicity, cultural fluency, and language skills. Leadership that exhibits this kind of two-dimensional (2D) diversity produces tangible results: employees at publicly-trading companies with 2D diversity are 70 percent more likely to report capturing a new market within the past twelve months as compared to companies lacking diversity, and 45 percent more likely to report that their company improved market share in the same time-frame (Sylvia Ann Hewlett, Melinda Marshall, and Laura Sherbin with Tara Gonzalves, *Innovation, Diversity, and Market Growth* (New York: Center for Talent Innovation, September 2013, 1-5).

7. Elliot and Sullivan, "Red Cross" (see note 1).

8. According to one study, the percentage of senior management roles held by expatriates in BRIC and Middle Eastern subsidiaries of MNCs dropped from 56 percent to 12 percent in the last decade (William J. Holstein, "The Decline of the Expat Executive," *Strategy + Business Magazine*, July 2008, 1, http://www.strategy-business.com/media/file/leading_ideas -20080729.pdf).

9. Justin Harper, "Expat Executives 'Squeezed Out' of China," *The Telegraph*, December 21, 2012, http://www.telegraph .co.uk/finance/personalfinance/expat-money/9755755/Expat -executives-squeezed-out-of-China.html.

10. Ashridge Business School, European Academy of Business in Society (EABIS), and United Nations Global Compact Principles for Responsible Management Education (PRME), *Developing the Global Leader of Tomorrow*, (Herfordshire, UK: Ashridge, 2013), 19, http://www.unprme.org/resource-docs /developingthegloballeaderoftomorrowreport.pdf. See also: Pankaj Ghemawat, "Developing Global Leaders," *McKinsey Quarterly*, June 2012, http://www.mckinsey.com/insights /leading_in_the_21st_century/developing_global_leaders.

11. J. R. Immelt, V. Govindarajan, and Chris Trimble, "How GE Is Disrupting Itself," *Harvard Business Review* 87, no.10 (2009), https://hbr.org/2009/10/how-ge-is-disrupting-itself.

12. Ibid.

13. Jena McGregor, "GE: Reinventing Tech for the Emerging World," *Bloomberg Business,* April 16, 2008, http://www.bloomberg

.com/bw/stories/2008-04-16/ge-reinventing-tech-for-the
-emerging-world.

14. Even in the case of GE, the initial idea for the ECG MAC 400 came
from HQ although the implementation was local (Ibid).

15. The most common way for US and European-based MNCs to
increase the diversity of their board of directors is through
cross-border mergers and acquisitions, rather than through
the promotion of local talent (Clifford Staples, "Board
Globalization in the World's Largest TNCs 1993-2005," *Corporate
Governance: An International Review* 15, no. 2 (2007): 318, doi:
10.1111/j.1467-8683.2007.00573.x).

16. While the cultural competency payoff of long-term assignment
abroad has long been acknowledged, recent research shows
that expatriate executives in US and European MNCs still take
significantly longer to climb the corporate ladder than those
based at HQ (Monika Hamori and Burak Koyuncu, "Career
Advancement in Large Organizations in Europe and the
United States: Do International Assignments Add Value?" *The
International Journal of Human Resource Management* 22, no. 4
(2011): 857, doi: 10.1080/09585192.2011.555128).

17. Pierre Gurdjian, Thomas Halbeisen, and Kevin Lane, "Why
Leadership-Development Programs Fail," McKinsey Quarterly,
January 2014, http://www.mckinsey.com/insights/leading_in
_the_21st_century/why_leadership-development_programs
_fail; Laci Loew and Karen O'Leonard, *Leadership Development
Factbook 2012: Benchmarks and Trends in U.S. Leadership
Development*, Bersin by Deloitte, July 2012; Douglas A. Ready
and Jay A. Conger, "Make Your Company a Talent Factory,"
Harvard Business Review 85, no. 6 (June 2007): 68-77.

18. John W. Bing, "Hofstede's Consequences: The Impact of His Work
on Consulting and Business Practices," *Academy of Management
Executive* 18, no. 1 (2004). For other consulting tools developed
in collaboration with the Hofstede's research, see: "Training
and Consulting," www.geerthofstede.nl, accessed July 10, 2015,
http://www.geerthofstede.nl/training--consulting.

19. Aperian Global, "GlobeSmart® Teaming Assessment," accessed
July 10, 2015, http://corp.aperianglobal.com/sites/default/files
/AG-MC-GTADatasheet_2013_111313-LTR.pdf.

20. For a fairly comprehensive list of organizations and consultancies
offering global cultural competency assessment and training

tools, see: "Intercultural Training and Assessment Tools," The Intercultural Communications Institute, accessed July 10, 2015, http://www.intercultural.org/documents/tools.pdf.

21. Geert Hofstede, "Cultural Constraints in Management Theories," *Academy of Management Executive* 7, no. 1 (February 1993): 81–94; Robert House, et al., *Culture, Leadership and Organizations: The GLOBE Study of 62 Societies*, (Thousand Oaks, CA: Sage Publications, 2004); Richard D. Lewis, *When Cultures Collide: Leading Across Cultures*, (Boston: Nicholas Brealey Publishing, 1996); Erin Meyer, *The Culture Map: Breaking Through the Invisible Boundaries of Global Business*, (New York: PublicAffairs, 2014); Ernest Gundling, *Working GlobeSmart: 12 People Skills for Doing Business across Borders*, (Mountain View, CA: Nicholas Brealey Publishing, 2011); Ernest Gundling, Terry Hogan and Karen Cvitkovich, *What is Global Leadership? 10 Key Behaviors That Define Great Global Leaders*, (Mountain View, CA: Nicholas Brealey Publishing, 2011).

22. The American Red Cross is a case in point. While their cultural outreach efforts, which included hiring an expert to train staff on cultural competency and making it "a priority to hire Haitians," look good on paper, in reality Haitian employees were rarely given the opportunity to climb to top positions in the Red Cross and their potential went untapped (Elliot and Sullivan, "Red Cross" (see note 1); see also: Simon Latraverse and Camoëns, "Mid Term Evaluation of the Gran Nò Pi Djanm Program," *American Red Cross Haiti Assistance Program,* March 2, 2015, 60, https://www.propublica.org/documents/item/2074306-internal-american-red-cross-evaluation-of-grand.html).

23. Kamel Mellahi and David G. Collings, "The Barriers to Effective Global Talent Management: The Example of Corporate Elites in MNEs," *Journal of World Business* 45, no. 2 (2010): 19-20, doi: 10.1016/j.jwb.2009.09.018; see also: Ron Boschma, "Proximity and Innovation: A Critical Assessment," *Regional Studies* 39, no.1 (2005).

24. Deloitte, "Tech Trends 2015: The Fusion of Business and IT," Deloitte University Press, 2015, http://d2mtr37y39tpbu.cloudfront.net/wp-content/uploads/2015/01/Tech-Trends-2015-FINAL_3.25.pdf.

25. IBM Institute for Business Value, "Leading Through Connections: Insights from the Global Chief Executive Officer Study," CEO C-Suite Studies Series, 2012, http://www-935.ibm.com/services/multimedia/anz_ceo_study_2012.pdf.

26. Towers Watson, "2015 HR Service Delivery and Technology Survey," June 2015, http://www.towerswatson.com/en-US /Insights/IC-Types/Survey-Research-Results/2015/05/2015-hr -service-delivery-and-technology-survey-results.

27. A Gartner report found that 42 percent of CIOs believe that their current organization lacks the key skills and capabilities necessary to respond to a complex digital business landscape. This digital skill deficit is further exacerbated by the fact that a majority of companies look to C-level or senior vice executives (37 percent and 44 percent respectively, according to a recent Forrester survey) to provide digital strategy leadership, rather than dedicated technology experts (Claudio Da Rold and Frances Karamouzis, "Digital Business Acceleration Elevates The Need For An Adaptive, Pace-Layered Sourcing Strategy," Gartner Inc., April 17, 2014; Martin Gill, "Predictions 2014: The Year of Digital Business," Forrester Research, Inc., December 19, 2013).

28. According to a recent Brookings report, 4.2 billion people remain unconnected to the Internet, many in key developing markets including Brazil, China, and India (Darrell M. West, "Digital Divide: Improving Internet Access in the Developing World through Affordable Services and Diverse Content," Center for Technology Innovation at Brookings, February 2015, http://www .brookings.edu/~/media/research/files/papers/2015/02/13 -digital-divide-developing-world-west/west_internet-access.pdf).

29. Virtual team management research shows that executives must also be comfortable adapting their leadership styles to the virtual environment to build trust and credibility in the absence of in-person interaction, although next to no research has directly addressed the added challenge of leading virtual teams across both geographic *and* cultural divides, a situation that is becoming more and more the norm. Interviews with executives, such as Marianna Waltz (associate managing director at Moody's in charge of Latin America), suggest that successful global leaders deploy limited in-person interactions to support and augment virtual teaming, but current research has yet to explore this important area. Significant contributions in the area of virtual team management and leadership include: Sirrka L. Jarvenpaa and Dorothy E. Leidner, "Communication and Trust in Global Virtual Teams," *Organization Science* 10, no. 6 (December 1999): doi: 1047-7039/99/1006/0791; Arvind Malhotra, Ann Majchrzak, and Benson Rosen, "Leading Virtual Teams," *Academy of Management Perspectives* 21, no. 1 (February 2007): 60-70,

doi: 10.5465/AMP.2007.24286164; Donald Davis and Janet Bryant, "Influence at a Distance: Leadership in Global Virtual Teams," *Advances in Global Leadership (Volume 3)*, (Bingley: Emerald Group, 2003), 303-340.

30. Sylvia Ann Hewlett, Noni Allwood, Karen Sumberg, and Sandra Scharf with Christina Fargnoli, *Cracking the Code: Executive Presence and Multicultural Professionals*, (New York: Center for Talent Innovation, November 2013); Sylvia Ann Hewlett, Melinda Marshall, and Laura Sherbin with Tara Gonsalves, *Innovation, Diversity, and Market Growth*, (New York: Center for Talent Innovation, September 2013).

31. Sylvia Ann Hewlett, with Kerrie Peraino, Laura Sherbin, and Karen Sumberg, *The Sponsor Effect*, (New York: Center for Talent Innovation, December 2010); Sylvia Ann Hewlett, *Forget a Mentor, Find a Sponsor: The New Way to Fast-Track Your Career*, (Cambridge: Harvard Business Review Press, 2013).

32. Sylvia Ann Hewlett, Melinda Marshall, and Laura Sherbin with Tara Gonsalves, *Innovation, Diversity, and Market Growth*, (New York: Center for Talent Innovation, 2013).

33. Sim Sitkin, "Learning Through Failure: The Strategy of Small Losses," *Research in Organizational Behavior* 14 (January 1992), 231-266.

34. Amy Edmondson, "Strategies for Learning from Failure," *Harvard Business Review*, April 2011, 55.

35. Rita Gunther McGrath, "Failing by Design," *Harvard Business Review*, April 2011, 79.

36. Edmondson, "Strategies," 52 (see note 29).

37. Name changed to protect source's anonymity.

38. Sylvia Ann Hewlett, Lauren Leader-Chivée, Karen Sumberg, Catherine Fredman, and Claire Ho, *Sponsor Effect: UK*, (New York: Center for Talent Innovation, 2012), 20.

39. Unpublished data from dataset published in: Sylvia Ann Hewlett, Melinda Marshall, Laura Sherbin, and Barbara Adachi, *The Sponsor Effect 2.0: Road Maps for Sponsors and Protégés*, (New York: Center for Talent Innovation, 2012).

METHODOLOGY

This research consists of a survey, Insights In-Depth® sessions (a proprietary web-based tool used to conduct voice-facilitated virtual focus groups) involving fifty-four people from our Task Force organizations, and one-on-one interviews with forty-eight men and women in Brazil, China, Hong Kong, India, Japan, Russia, Singapore, South Africa, Turkey, the US, and the UK.

Survey data comes from two large-scale samples of college educated respondents over the age of twenty-one currently employed full-time. Survey One, conducted online between November 2014 and April 2015, includes 12,029 men and women (1,005 in Brazil; 1,005 in China; 1,001 in Hong Kong; 1,004 in India; 1,004 in Japan; 1,001 in Russia; 1,001 in Singapore; 1,002 in South Africa; 1,003 in Turkey; 1,003 in the UK; and 2,000 in the US). Survey Two, conducted online in May 2015, includes 6,014 men and women (1,007 in Brazil; 1,001 in China; 1,001 in Hong Kong; 1,000 in India; 1,004 in the UK; and 1,001 in the US). Data were weighted on gender, age, income, and ethnicity in the US, and gender and age in all other countries. Survey One had an additional weight to be balanced across all countries. The base used for statistical testing was the effective base.

The survey was conducted by GMI Lightspeed under the auspices of the Center for Talent Innovation, a nonprofit research organization. GMI Lightspeed was responsible for the data collection, while the Center for Talent Innovation conducted the analysis.

ACKNOWLEDGMENTS

The authors are deeply grateful to the study sponsors and those who have been integral to the research's success: Valerie Grillo and Anré Williams at American Express; Erika Irish Brown, David Tamburelli, and Elana Weinstein at Bloomberg; Cassandra Frangos and Shari Slate at Cisco; Karyn Twaronite at EY; Piyush Mehta and "Tiger" Tyagarajan at Genpact; Caroline Carr at Goldman Sachs; Rosalind Hudnell at Intel; Gail Fierstein and Melinda Wolfe at Pearson; Rohini Anand at Sodexo; and Frances G. Laserson at The Moody's Foundation.

We are grateful to the rest of our cochairs as well—Redia Anderson, Deborah Elam, Patricia Fili-Krushel, Trevor Gandy, David Gonzales, Wanda Hope, Renee Johnson, Patricia Langer, Keri Matthews, Kendall O'Brien, Lisa Garcia Quiroz, Craig Robinson, Sarah St. Clair, Eileen Taylor, and Geri Thomas—for their vision and commitment.

We are grateful to Tai Wingfield and Lisa Weinert for spearheading the publication of this report as a book, the first of a series of CTI books. We deeply appreciate the efforts of the rest of the CTI team, specifically Joseph Cervone, Kennedy Ihezie, Deidra Mascoll, and

Peggy Shiller. Thanks also to Noni Allwood, Carolyn Buck Luce, Terri Chung, Mark Fernandez, Jessica Jia, Lawrence Jones, Andrea Turner Moffitt, Ripa Rashid, Sandra Scharf, Joan Snyder Kuhl, and Brandon Urquhart for their support. We also appreciate the support provided by our interns, Joel Jean-Claude Alexander, Catherine Chapman, Randy Clinton, Zachary Insani, and Douglas Molina.

Thanks to the private-sector members of the Task Force for Talent Innovation for their practical ideas and collaborative energy: Elaine Aarons, Rachael Akohonae, Jolen Anderson, Renee Anderson, Antoine Andrews, Diane Ashley, Nadine Augusta, Jane Ayaduray, Ken Barrett, Tony Byers, Myrna Chao, Kenneth Charles, Jyoti Chopra, Elise Clarke, Tanya Clemons, Fiona Daniel, Nancy Di Dia, Lisa Dzintars-Pahwul, Traci Entel, Nicole Erb, Hedieh Fakhriyazdi, Grace Figueredo, Kent Gardiner, Heide Gardner, Peter Gaytan, Lisa George, James Gibbs, Tina Gilbert, Marc Grainger, Michele Green, Lisa Gutierrez, Kathleen Hart, Neesha Hathi, Maja Hazell, Jessica Heffron, Kara Helander, Celia Pohani Huber, Bill Huffaker, Sylvia James, Cecily Joseph, Nia Joynson-Romanzina, Panagiotis Karahalios, Shannon Kelleher, Rosemarie Lanard, Maja Lehnus, Janice Little, Cynthia Marshall, Lori Massad, Ana Duarte McCarthy, Beth McCormick, Mark McLane, Sylvester Mendoza, Kristen Mleczko, Terilyn Monroe, Loren Monroe-Trice, Meredith Moore, Christal Morris, Leena Nair, Janell Nelson, Elizabeth Nieto,

Pamela Norley, Jennifer O'Lear, Cindy Pace, Monica Parham, Jimmie Paschall, Cara Peck, Donna Pedro, Hy Pomerance, Danyale Price, Susan Reid, Eiry Wyn Roberts, Dwight Robinson, Christine Rogers-Raetsch, Aida Sabo, Sue Schmidlkofer, Belinda Shannon, Meisha Sherman, Maria Stolfi, Karen Sumberg, Brian Tippens, Vera Vitels, Lynn O'Connor Vos, Barbara Wankoff, Amy Whitley, and Nadia Younes.

Thanks also to Paul Abbott, Zaid Al-Hadhrami, Karen Attyah, Koenrad Bastiaens, Lena Bjurner, Elaine Bonner, Paul Burton, Connie Bustamante, Sonia Cargan, Janet Chan, Jenny Chan, Melanie Cochrane, Timothy Coogan, Marco Croci, Jodi Davidson, John Donovan, Lisa Douglas, Katie Dowbiggin, Makiko Eda, Vasantha Erraguntla, Joanna Fang, Edwina Fitzmaurice, Gianni Giacomelli, Ehrika Gladden, Isabel Gomez-Vidal, Sherry Greenfield, Nicole Grozinski, Joanne Hannaford, Paul Hardoin, Andrea Harris, Ike Harris, Pascal Henssen, Satu Heschung, Russell Hoch, Matt Jahansouz, Melissa James, Nicolas Japy, Raymond Joabar, Yat Chung Koh, Michael Koons, Annie Kurian, Inbar Lasser-Raab, Ron Lee, Frank Lento, Waishan Leung, Andres Maz, Kerrie McPherson, Satya-Christophe Menard, Sylvia Metayer, Rebecca Midura, Tamara Minick-Scokalo, Sunil Nayak, Mathieu Oudot, Edzard Overbeek, Sanjay Pal, Kerrie Peraino, Lisa Peschke-Koedt, Hasan Rafiq, Saravan Rajendran, Janet Ramey, Philippe Sachs, Alessandra Sapiz, Suzanne Schaeffer, Susanne Seefeldt, Christophe Solas, Diana Solash,

Lorenzo Soriano, Kumud Srinivasan, Claudia Subirat, Juan Pablo Urritocoechea, Jim Walsh, Marianna Waltz, Liz Wamai, Carole Watkins, Dave Womelsdorf, Sam Xu, and the women and men who took part in Insights In-Depth® sessions.

ADDITIONAL PUBLICATIONS

KEEPING TALENTED WOMEN ON THE ROAD TO SUCCESS

The Power of the Purse: Engaging Women Decision Makers for Healthy Outcomes
Sponsors: Aetna, Bristol-Myers Squibb, Cardinal Health, Eli Lilly and Company, Johnson & Johnson, Merck & Co., Merck KGaA, MetLife, Pfizer, PwC, Strategy&, Teva, WPP (2015)

Women Want Five Things
Sponsors: American Express, AT&T, Bank of America, Boehringer Ingelheim USA, Merck KGaA, The Moody's Foundation (2014)

Harnessing the Power of the Purse: Female Investors and Global Opportunities for Growth
Sponsors: Credit Suisse, Deutsche Bank, Goldman Sachs, Morgan Stanley, Standard Chartered Bank, UBS (2014)

Executive Presence: The Missing Link Between Merit and Success
HarperCollins, June 2014

Forget a Mentor, Find a Sponsor: The New Way to Fast-Track Your Career
Harvard Business Review Press, September 2013

On-Ramps and Up-Ramps India
Sponsors: Citi, Genpact, Sodexo, Standard Chartered Bank, Unilever (2013)

Executive Presence
Sponsors: American Express, Bloomberg LP, Credit Suisse, Ernst & Young, Gap Inc., Goldman Sachs, Interpublic Group, The Moody's Foundation (2012)

Sponsor Effect 2.0: Road Maps for Sponsors and Protégés
Sponsors: American Express, AT&T, Booz Allen Hamilton, Deloitte, Freddie Mac, Genentech, Morgan Stanley (2012)

Sponsor Effect: UK
Sponsor: Lloyds Banking Group (2012)

Off-Ramps and On-Ramps Japan: Keeping Talented Women on the Road to Success
Sponsors: Bank of America, Cisco, Goldman Sachs (2011)

The Relationship You Need to Get Right
Harvard Business Review, October 2011

Sponsor Effect: Breaking Through the Last Glass Ceiling
Sponsors: American Express, Deloitte, Intel, Morgan Stanley (2010)

Off-Ramps and On-Ramps Revisited
Harvard Business Review, June 2010

Off-Ramps and On-Ramps Revisited
Sponsors: Cisco, Ernst & Young, The Moody's Foundation (2010)

Letzte Ausfahrt Babypause
Harvard Business Manager (Germany), May 2010

Off-Ramps and On-Ramps Germany
Sponsors: Boehringer Ingelheim, Deutsche Bank, Siemens AG (2010)

Off-Ramps and On-Ramps: Keeping Talented Women on the Road to Success
Harvard Business Review Press, 2007

Off-Ramps and On-Ramps: Keeping Talented Women on the Road to Success
Harvard Business Review, March 2005

The Hidden Brain Drain: Off-Ramps and On-Ramps in Women's Careers
Sponsors: Ernst & Young, Goldman Sachs, Lehman Brothers (2005)

LEVERAGING MINORITY AND MULTICULTURAL TALENT

Black Women: Ready to Lead
Sponsors: American Express, AT&T, Bank of America, Chubb Group of Insurance Companies, Intel, Morgan Stanley, The Depository Trust & Clearing Corporation, White & Case LLP (2015)

How Diversity Drives Innovation: A Compendium of Best Practices
Sponsors: Bloomberg LP, Bristol-Myers Squibb, Cisco, Deutsche Bank, EY, Siemens AG, Time Warner (2014)

Cracking the Code: Executive Presence and Multicultural Professionals
Sponsors: Bank of America, Chubb Group of Insurance Companies, Deloitte, GE, Intel Corporation, McKesson Corporation (2013)

How Diversity Can Drive Innovation
Harvard Business Review, December 2013

Innovation, Diversity and Market Growth
Sponsors: Bloomberg LP, Bristol-Myers Squibb, Cisco, Deutsche Bank, EY, Siemens AG, Time Warner (2013)

Vaulting the Color Bar: How Sponsorship Levers Multicultural Professionals into Leadership
Sponsors: American Express, Bank of America, Bristol-Myers Squibb, Deloitte, Intel, Morgan Stanley, NBCUniversal (2012)

Asians in America: Unleashing the Potential of the "Model Minority"
Sponsors: Deloitte, Goldman Sachs, Pfizer, Time Warner (2011)

Sin Fronteras: Celebrating and Capitalizing on the Strengths of Latina Executives
Sponsors: Booz Allen Hamilton, Cisco, Credit Suisse, General Electric, Goldman Sachs, Johnson & Johnson, Time Warner (2007)

Global Multicultural Executives and the Talent Pipeline
Sponsors: Citigroup, General Electric, PepsiCo, Time Warner, Unilever (2008)

Leadership in Your Midst: Tapping the Hidden Strengths of Minority Executives
Harvard Business Review, November 2005

Invisible Lives: Celebrating and Leveraging Diversity in the Executive Suite
Sponsors: General Electric, Time Warner, Unilever (2005)

REALIZING THE FULL POTENTIAL OF LGBT TALENT

The Power of "Out"2.0: LGBT in the Workplace
Sponsors: Deloitte, Out on the Street, Time Warner (2013)

For LGBT Workers, Being "Out" Brings Advantages
Harvard Business Review, July/August 2011

The Power of "Out": LGBT in the Workplace
Sponsors: American Express, Boehringer Ingelheim USA, Cisco, Credit Suisse, Deloitte, Google (2011)

Forthcoming 2016: *LGBT Equality: The Power of "Out" on the Global Stage*

RETAINING AND SUSTAINING TOP TALENT

Top Talent: Keeping Performance Up When Business Is Down
Harvard Business Press, 2009

Sustaining High Performance in Difficult Times
Sponsor: The Moody's Foundation (2008)

Seduction and Risk: The Emergence of Extreme Jobs
Sponsors: American Express, BP plc, ProLogis, UBS (2007)

Extreme Jobs: The Dangerous Allure of the 70-Hour Workweek
Harvard Business Review, December 2006

TAPPING INTO THE STRENGTHS OF GEN Y, GEN X, AND BOOMERS

The X Factor: Tapping into the Strengths of the 33- to 46-Year-Old Generation
Sponsors: American Express, Boehringer Ingelheim USA, Cisco, Credit Suisse, Google (2011)

How Gen Y & Boomers Will Reshape Your Agenda
Harvard Business Review, July/August 2009

Bookend Generations: Leveraging Talent and Finding Common Ground
Sponsors: Booz Allen Hamilton, Ernst & Young, Lehman Brothers, Time Warner, UBS (2009)

BECOMING A TALENT MAGNET IN EMERGING MARKETS

The Battle for Female Talent in Brazil
Sponsors: Bloomberg LP, Booz & Company, Intel, Pfizer, Siemens AG (2011)

Winning the War for Talent in Emerging Markets
Harvard Business Press, August 2011

The Battle for Female Talent in China
Sponsors: Bloomberg LP, Booz & Company, Intel, Pfizer,
Siemens AG (2010)

The Battle for Female Talent in India
Sponsors: Bloomberg LP, Booz & Company, Intel, Pfizer,
Siemens AG (2010)

The Battle for Female Talent in Emerging Markets
Harvard Business Review, May 2010

Preventing the Exodus of Women in Set

Athena Factor 2.0: Accelerating Female Talent in Science,
Engineering & Technology
Sponsors: American Express, Boehringer Ingelheim USA,
BP, Genentech, McKesson Corporation, Merck Serono,
Schlumberger, Siemens AG (2014)

The Under-Leveraged Talent Pool: Women Technologists on
Wall Street
Sponsors: Bank of America, Credit Suisse, Goldman Sachs,
Intel, Merrill Lynch, NYSE Euronext (2008)

Stopping the Exodus of Women in Science
Harvard Business Review, June 2008

The Athena Factor: Reversing the Brain Drain in Science,
Engineering, and Technology
Sponsors: Alcoa, Cisco, Johnson & Johnson, Microsoft, Pfizer
(2008)

TASK FORCE FOR TALENT INNOVATION

Co-Chairs

American Express

Bank of America

Bloomberg

Booz Allen Hamilton

BP

Bristol-Myers Squibb

Chubb Group of Insurance Companies

Cisco Systems

Deutsche Bank

Ernst & Young LLP

GE

Goldman Sachs

Intel Corporation

Johnson & Johnson

NBCUniversal

Pearson

Time Warner

Members

Aetna

AllianceBernstein

AT&T

Baker Botts LLP

Barclays PLC

BlackRock

BNP Paribas

BNY Mellon

Boehringer Ingelheim USA

BT Group**

Cardinal Health

Central Intelligence Agency

Charles Schwab & Co.

Citi**

Credit Suisse**

Crowell & Moring LLP

The Depository Trust & Clearing Corporation

Eli Lilly and Company

Federal Reserve Bank of New York

Fidelity Investments

Freddie Mac

General Mills

General Motors

Genpact

GlaxoSmithKline

Google

Hewlett-Packard

HSBC Bank PLC

Intercontinental Exchange/
NYSE

International Monetary Fund

Interpublic Group

Intuit

KPMG LLP

McGraw Hill Financial

McKesson Corporation

McKinsey & Company

Merck*

MetLife

Morgan Stanley

Northrop Grumman

Novartis Pharmaceuticals
Corp.

Ogilvy & Mather

PAREXEL International

Paul, Weiss, Rifkind,
Wharton & Garrison LLP

Pfizer Inc.**

Pratt & Whitney

Prudential Financial

QBE North America

Sodexo

Standard Chartered Bank

Starbucks

Strategy&

Swiss Reinsurance Co.

Symantec

Teva

The Moody's Foundation**

Thomson Reuters

Towers Watson

UBS**

Unilever PLC

UPS

Vanguard

Visa

Weil, Gotshal & Manges LLP

Wells Fargo and Company

White & Case LLP

Withers LLP

Wounded Warrior Project

WPP

*Merck KGaA (Darmstadt, Germany)

** Steering Committee

As of August 2015

INDEX

ABOUT THE AUTHORS

Sylvia Ann Hewlett is the founder and CEO of the Center for Talent Innovation and Hewlett Consulting Partners LLC. A Cambridge-trained economist, her research focuses on global talent management and the retention and acceleration of highly qualified women and other previously excluded groups. She is the author of twelve critically acclaimed books, including *Forget a Mentor, Find a Sponsor* (Harvard Business Review Press, 2013) and *Executive Presence* (Harper Business, 2014). Hewlett has taught at Columbia and Princeton universities. In 2014, the European Diversity Awards honored her with its Global Diversity Award.

Ripa Rashid, managing partner at Hewlett Consulting Partners LLC and senior vice president at the Center for Talent Innovation, specializes in global talent strategies and has spent over a decade as a management consultant. She has held senior positions at MetLife and Time Warner. A graduate of Harvard University and INSEAD's MBA program, she has lived and worked in North America, Europe, Asia, and South America, and speaks four languages. She is coauthor, with Hewlett, of *Winning the War for Talent in Emerging Markets: Why Women Are the Solution* (Harvard Business Review Press, 2011).

CPSIA information can be obtained at www.ICGtesting.com
Printed in the USA
BVOW08s0402160316

440510BV00003B/17/P